Reflecting in Communities of Practice

Other Redleaf Press Books by Deb Curtis and Margie Carter

The Art of Awareness: How Observation Can Transform Your Teaching, second edition

Designs for Living and Learning: Transforming Early Childhood Environments

Learning Together with Young Children: A Curriculum Framework for Reflective Teachers

Reflecting Children's Lives: A Handbook for Planning Your Child-Centered Curriculum, second edition

Training Teachers: A Harvest of Theory and Practice

The Visionary Director: A Handbook for Dreaming, Organizing, and Improvising in Your Center, second edition

Reflecting
in Communities of Practice

A WORKBOOK FOR EARLY CHILDHOOD EDUCATORS

DEB CURTIS · DEBBIE LEBO · WENDY C. M. CIVIDANES · MARGIE CARTER

Redleaf Press®
www.redleafpress.org
800-423-8309

Published by Redleaf Press
10 Yorkton Court
St. Paul, MN 55117
www.redleafpress.org

First edition 2013
Cover design by Jim Handrigan
Cover photograph © Fancy Photography/Veer
Interior design by Erin Kirk New
Typeset in Minion Pro
Interior photographs by Deb Curtis except on page 38, by Debbie Lebo
Illustrations on page 63 by Barbara J. Massam
Printed in the United States of America

The sections entitled "What Is Reflective Teaching," "A Reflective Teacher at Work," and "I'm Incredible: A Story by Deb Curtis" on pages 6–8 are adapted from "Becoming a Reflective Teacher" by Margie Carter, Wendy Cividanes, Deb Curtis, and Debbie Lebo (*Teaching Young Children* 3[4]: 18–20), © 2010 by the National Association for the Education of Young Children. Adapted with permission.

Library of Congress Cataloging-in-Publication Data
Curtis, Deb.
   Reflecting in communities of practice : a workbook for early childhood educators / Deb Curtis, Debbie Lebo, Wendy C. M. Cividanes, and Margie Carter.
      pages cm
   Includes bibliographical references.
   ISBN 978-1-60554-148-8 (pbk. : alk. paper)
   ISBN 978-1-60554-259-1 (e-book)
   1. Early childhood education—Curricula—United States. 2. Early childhood education—Activity programs—United States. 3. Reflective teaching—United States. 4. Professional learning communities.   I. Title.
   LB1139.4.C89 2013
   372.21—dc23
                        2013001770

Printed on acid-free paper   U15-04

This workbook is dedicated to the people who have been members of our communities of practice and our critical friends, with special appreciation for one another and our fellow Harvest Resources Associates.

CONTENTS

ACKNOWLEDGMENTS

We'd like to thank the many people who contributed stories, examples, and photos to this workbook, including Lorrie Baird and the staff of Kawartha Child Care Services; the Burlington Little School; Martin Luther King Day Home Center; United Way Bright Beginnings in Houston, Texas; Christie Colunga and colleagues at Paradise Valley Community College; Laura McAllister and Sound Child Care Solutions; Valerie Rajotte and Montgomery Child Care Association; Anne Hentschel; Kristie Norwood; and Ijumaa Jordan. We also thank our early childhood colleagues in New Zealand for inspiring us with their work on learning stories and professional development.

We are very grateful to David Heath, Carla Valadez, and the entire Redleaf Press team for their insights and skills.

And we give a special thanks to our families for their patience, understanding, and continued support.

Introduction

Imagine you're heading into your work as an early childhood professional—what is on your mind? Are you feeling energized and excited, eager to see children, families, and coworkers? Are you ready to embark together on the day's learning expedition? Or are other, less positive, ideas creeping into your thoughts?

- Are you being pulled away from your focus on the children by a tide of paperwork, regulations, and assessments?

- Are you in a stressful tug-of-war with time, trying to stay present in the moment with the children as you pack all your program's required activities into your daily routine?

- Do you find yourself getting bogged down in the role of "early childhood police officer," with your attention grabbed by behavior problems and conflict management?

- Are you feeling isolated and alone in your work? Do you long for an opportunity to talk through your professional delights, struggles, and ongoing questions? Are you seeking a trusted colleague who understands and respects your point of view?

- When you work with teachers to improve their practice, do you find that they simply want to be told what to do? That they'd rather not have to think through the teaching and learning process?

If you're like most early childhood professionals, we suspect you feel some combination of these thoughts and feelings on a regular basis. As a teacher, family child care provider, administrator, or teacher educator, you already know that it is a challenging time to be working in this field. You probably came into this profession with a vision of supporting children's joyful learning and development. You, like us, feel the pulls and pressures of so many factors conspiring against that vision. With all of this in mind, let's start with a couple of simple questions:

- What do you deserve to feel as you head into work each day?
- What would make you feel more successful and joyful in your work?

Taking a Stand for Reflective Teaching

We believe that reflective teaching stems from a deep respect for the complexity of teaching and learning. Reflective early childhood teachers are intentional and thoughtful about their beliefs and practices, and they continuously review and analyze their observations and experiences with young children. They use their reflections in and out of the classroom to take actions that steadily improve their professional teaching practice. Reflective early childhood teacher educators, coaches, mentors, and administrators engage in a parallel process when they study observations of children alongside teachers and give careful consideration to teachers' thinking and learning.

Reflective teaching is hardly a new concept. A century ago, progressive educator John Dewey (1910) wrote about the importance of reflection in the teaching and learning process. For Dewey, reflection was a way for teachers to reorganize their thinking, to look at all sides of a situation, and to avoid the impulse to keep doing the same old things in the same old ways.

Like Dewey, we see reflection as a key component of responsive, deeply child-centered teaching. Because each child and each teaching situation is unique, effective teachers must continuously reflect on their reactions to everything that happens in the classroom. No single set of strategies or techniques can work for all teachers, with all children, or in all circumstances. Instead, teaching requires a mind-set of constant, sensitive, skillful, and reflective decision making, both in and out of the action of the classroom. Teachers need and *deserve* time and guidance to support this process.

So what does it mean to be a reflective early childhood professional in today's world? The standards and accountability movement that swept over the entire US educational system during the last decade has now taken solid hold in the early childhood community. Program administrators feel pressure to demonstrate accountability to rising standards by adopting teacher-proof curricula. Teachers resort to one-size-fits-all teaching techniques in order to comply with regulations and mandates. Quality Rating Improvement Systems (QRIS) are adding more high-stakes assessment tools, but teachers are rarely guided to use these tools as resources for self-reflection. The trend toward more standardization without daily support systems for teachers directly threatens reflective teaching practices. Even more, prescriptive, mechanical teaching approaches start to drain the joy and passion from working with young children, leaving teachers feeling frustrated, burnt-out, and diminished as professionals.

We don't find fault with most early childhood standards in and of themselves. Standards can serve as valuable benchmarks for defining equitable expectations for best practices in early childhood programs. Our concern is that so few early childhood programs are establishing systems and structures so teachers and administrators can collaboratively reflect on, understand, and integrate standards into their daily work in an illuminating way. Without such forums for shared reflection, standards can easily become meaningless requirements. Teaching is reduced to a scripted, rote practice that demeans the complexity of young children's learning and development. Teachers begin to feel like preprogrammed technicians instead of capable and competent professionals.

We believe early childhood teachers deserve to head into work each day feeling fully absorbed in and enthusiastic about learning—the children's and their own. We want teacher educators, coaches, mentors, and administrators to look beyond checklists of teacher competencies and to encourage dispositions of curiosity and engagement. At a time when so much energy is focused on educational standardization, compliance, and prescription, we want to stand for teachers' right to exercise creative, critical, and reflective thinking in their work.

An Alternative to Standardization: Teaching as Research

Our goal in writing this workbook is to offer an alternate approach—to enhance quality by supporting early childhood teachers as reflective practitioners. Ultimately, it is the minute-to-minute, hour-to-hour, day-to-day choices of teachers that have the most impact on the quality of children's learning experience. Whatever your role or setting in the early childhood field, we hope this workbook will reenergize you and reinforce your identity as a reflective professional. We want to inspire you to create new possibilities for supporting and thinking through the complexity of your work with others who are, in Louise Boyd Cadwell's (2003, 25) words, "always listening for a surprise and the birth of a new idea."

As you engage in the experiences in this workbook, we hope you will strengthen your image of yourself as a thinker and generator of knowledge, not just a consumer of other people's thinking. We have been inspired by a growing body of research and the work of educators in Reggio Emilia, Italy, and Aotearoa/New Zealand to look at early childhood teaching as research (Gallas 2003; Meier and Henderson 2007; Rinaldi 2006). For teacher-researchers, an ongoing cycle of inquiry, observation, data collection, and reflection is a natural part of daily interactions with children.

From a teacher-researcher's point of view, reflection is more than just informal thinking or talking with others about your work; it is an essential part of your teaching practice. You set aside specific time alone or with others to engage in reflection as a systematic process. William Ayers (2004, 110) describes it this way: "Reflection is thinking rigorously, critically, and systematically about practices and problems of importance to further growth. . . . Reflection is a disciplined way of assessing situations, imagining a future different from today, and preparing to act."

This view of reflection is one that can inspire and excite you as an early childhood professional, one that becomes not a drain on your time but rather a source of intellectual engagement and new energy.

The Value of Reflection

Learning to be a reflective teacher is a valuable investment that pays off practically in your day-to-day work. It strengthens your image of children and your ability to think through and act on the complex issues you continually face in your program. Reflection keeps you a lifelong learner. It helps you take a stand for

- staying true to the values you want to bring to your work;
- being the teacher you want to be; and
- providing the learning environment you want for young children and their families.

Whether you are a family child care provider, a teacher, an administrator, a coach, a mentor, or a teacher educator, we hope you will use this workbook as a study tool for yourself and with others to strengthen your ability to work with integrity and a strong identity as a reflective professional.

CHAPTER 1

Are You a Reflective Teacher?

Assess Yourself

Take some time to think about yourself and your approach to working with children. Use the following self-assessment to help focus your thoughts.

Are You a Reflective Teacher?

Assess yourself using the following elements of reflective teaching. Respond to each statement by writing *always, often, sometimes, rarely,* or *never.*

_____ 1.   I examine my own reactions to children and their actions to understand their source.

_____ 2.   I am curious about children's play and watch it closely.

_____ 3.   I document details of children's conversations and activities.

_____ 4.   I take time to study notes and photos to puzzle out what's significant.

_____ 5.   I eagerly share stories about children's learning with families and coworkers.

_____ 6.   I ask coworkers and children's families for their insights.

_____ 7.   I read professional literature to learn more.

_____ 8.   I show children photos and stories of themselves to hear their views.

_____ 9.   I use my observations and reflections to change the environment and materials to encourage new play and learning possibilities.

Adapted from *Reflecting Children's Lives: A Handbook for Planning Your Child-Centered Curriculum,* second edition, by Deb Curtis and Margie Carter, © 2011. Published by Redleaf Press, www.redleafpress.org.

What Is Reflective Teaching?

Teaching young children is complex work. Every day, teachers face many challenges—the ongoing chores of caregiving and cleanup, planning and providing an engaging curriculum, communicating with families and coworkers, and responding to the ever-growing pressures for outcomes, assessment, and documentation to demonstrate children's learning.

These pressures compete for teachers' attention, making it difficult to keep the joy of being with children at the heart of their work. Teachers can turn to the many resources available to learn about guidance techniques or they can use a published curriculum to help with planning. Coaches, administrators, or teacher educators might provide tips, strategies, and technical assistance to help teachers comply with standards. Yet to truly share meaningful experiences with children, teachers must strive to become reflective thinkers, eager to puzzle through their role in supporting children's learning, identity development, and sense of belonging.

For reflective teachers, work is an ongoing process of closely observing and studying the significance of unfolding activities. Rather than just following preplanned lessons and techniques, reflective teachers consider what they know about the particular children in their group. They apply their knowledge of child development theory to better understand and delight in what happens in the classroom. Reflection allows teachers to make effective, meaningful decisions about how to respond to and plan for children. Reflective teaching keeps teachers excited about their work.

A Reflective Teacher at Work

In the following story you will read how Deb has become a reflective teacher. She uses the Learning Story format from Aotearoa/New Zealand. Following this approach, the story is written to a particular child. The story describes the details of the child's recent activity and the teacher's interest in and thinking about the significance of the event for the child's learning. Also notice that Deb invites the child's family to share their knowledge and ideas.

"I'm Incredible": A Story by Deb Curtis

Jacob, a few weeks ago you came up to me and said, "I'm incredible!" I was delighted and responded that of course you are incredible. I realized that you were trying out your newly discovered incredible imagination. Over the first months of preschool you have been pretending you are someone different every day. It is amazing to watch you become a firefighter or a tiger. You use the dress-up clothes and props to enhance these dramatic moments. Your friends love your new ideas and follow you in this make-believe play.

Sometimes your big energy and loud voices make me nervous that someone might get hurt. Last week you found the shovel and decided it was a sword and you were a knight. You ran around the yard with swashbuckling grace, waving your sword. Your friends were excited as they joined you in this drama. I told you to make sure you were just pretending, so you wouldn't hurt anyone. You assured me a few times: "This is real, but I won't hurt anyone."

My reflections on what your play means

I am thrilled to watch you realize the power of your imagination. You *are* incredible—a smart thinker with a huge vocabulary—so it makes sense that you use these gifts in powerful ways. It is also wonderful that you and your friends are able to share in this play together. Playing together in this way is new for all of you. Through this kind of play you are learning social skills and cooperation. Understanding the importance of this play for you eases my concern over your big energy. I know that my first reaction to this kind of play is often about safety. But I also know that this is the beginning of years of pretend play during which you and your friends will make up many adventures. And this kind of dramatic play is an important way for you to develop language skills and creative thinking that will support all your future learning.

My thoughts about opportunities your play provides

I'll continue to provide more props to support your dramatic play. I'll observe, document, and create books about your play to read back to you and your friends. I'll keep showing your ideas to the other children so you can help them learn the power of their imaginations! I will pause and notice my first reactions to your play to determine if my worries about safety are founded. We will continue to negotiate together this active play that is so important to you while making sure you keep yourself and others safe.

Questions for Jacob's family

What pretend play does Jacob enjoy at home? What is your view of his active, loud play? How do you support him in staying safe? I'm eager to hear your stories.

Think about Deb's Reflections

Deb's reflections about her observations of Jacob's actions help her to take his play seriously. She notes her own reactions: delight in Jacob's lively imagination and concern about safety. If she didn't reflect on the larger significance of this play, she might stop it because of her discomfort. Her descriptions show how she continues to think through her goals and values, attending to children's safety while appreciating and supporting these energetic and valuable activities. She is eager to ask Jacob's family's to tell her what they have seen him do at home and how they handle it. The information they provide will expand her understanding of Jacob and lead to meaningful two-way information sharing between home and school.

Characteristics of Reflective Teaching

What sets reflective teachers apart from other teachers? What characteristics do they display? Six basic characteristics are shared by teachers who practice reflective teaching:

1. Reflective teachers ask themselves questions.

2. Reflective teachers consider children's perspectives.

3. Reflective teachers are eager to gain more perspectives.

4. Reflective teachers look for details.

5. Reflective teachers examine the environment.

6. Reflective teachers are fully engaged in their work.

Reflective Teachers Ask Themselves Questions

As you read in Deb's story and her thoughts about Jacob, the heart of reflective teaching is taking time to think and respond rather than reacting without larger considerations. Reflective teachers ask themselves questions, first to reflect on their own responses to any situation and then to consider what from their own experiences and beliefs might be influencing their responses. Before reacting from this personal place, they consider whether their point of view will support or detract from the children's experience. Reflective teachers are willing to examine themselves, and they have a clear sense of what they value and the role they play in children's lives.

Reflective Teachers Consider Children's Perspectives

Reflective teachers believe that children are competent thinkers and learners and that their ideas and actions are worth taking seriously. They notice the details of children's activities to learn more about what might be on children's minds. Reflective teachers see themselves as researchers of the teaching and learning process. They work side by side with children in deepening understandings.

Reflective Teachers Are Eager to Gain More Perspectives

Reflective teachers also seek out many perspectives to enhance their understandings of their work. They are eager to interact and share stories of children with coworkers and the children's families. They spend time studying theories about children and child development to consider how theory connects to their daily practices with children.

Reflective Teachers Look for Details

Observing children closely and noticing the details of how they engage with materials and each other are critical practices for reflective teaching. The details of what is unfolding with children become the data that reflective teachers use to study the teaching and learning process.

Reflective Teachers Examine the Environment

Reflective teachers understand that the environment and materials play a powerful role in enhancing the teaching and learning process, so they continually assess and consider the impact of the environment and adapt and change it to enhance children's experiences.

Reflective Teachers Are Fully Engaged in Their Work

For reflective teachers, working with children is a journey filled with joys and struggles that lead to an engaged and nourishing professional life. Most of all, reflective teachers delight in children and the amazing learning and development unfolding around all of them, both teachers and children.

Reflecting on My Work

Do any of these ideas resonate with you? Circle the responses that do.

I'm an early childhood teacher.

I think of my work as

very significant	very stimulating

It's as if I'm

an air traffic controller, trying to keep everyone on a track and prevent collisions	a gardener, tilling the soil and planting the seeds for a love of learning

I spend hours

filling out forms and filling out the required documentation, not to mention getting materials ready for activities	thinking and reflecting on what has unfolded in my room and what I can do next with the children

There's so little time

and we have to take advantage of every moment so children can learn the skills that will help them feel good about themselves in school	for children to play and slip into the wonder of childhood, to splash through puddles, feel powerful in their bodies, and pursue their questions in meaningful ways

I need time

to go to workshops and get new ideas for activities and strategies for classroom management

to study my observations with coworkers so we can learn what's on the children's minds and plan around that

What I really need for my professional development is

a clear explanation of how all these standards and requirements are going to make my job easier

an opportunity to talk with others and think through the complexities of the teaching and learning process

I wish I had someone

at my side to help me when things aren't going well

to be a helpful mentor, but only if she is a good listener and respects what I'm trying to do

I need help

figuring out what to do with the difficult kids in my room

remembering that every child is competent and finding and respecting each child's point of view

I really feel grateful

when people understand how hard my job is

when people understand the bigger vision and importance of my work

Adapted from *The Art of Awareness: How Observation Can Transform Your Teaching*, second edition, by Deb Curtis and Margie Carter, © 2013. Published by Redleaf Press, www.redleafpress.org.

CHAPTER 2

A Model to Support Reflective Teaching

What are you longing for in your professional learning? Take a few minutes to talk with a colleague or jot down some of your thoughts.

_____

_____

_____

_____

_____

_____

_____

When it comes to professional learning, here are some of the deeper longings we often hear from early childhood professionals:

- time to think without rushing
- opportunities to talk regularly with a small group of people who do the same kind of work
- someone who cares about them and helps them consider other perspectives
- a framework to focus their thinking, organize their ideas, and make effective decisions

As you think about your days with children, how do you currently sort through all the complexities of your work? Maybe you spend time on your own, puzzling over the challenging moments or delighting in the children's learning. Most likely you grab a quick minute in the bathroom or staff room (if you have one) to talk with a coworker about your wonderings or your struggles. If you're lucky, you may have a bit of time in staff meetings to talk together about your work. You might also eagerly go to a workshop or conference looking for some ideas and quick solutions to some of the challenges you face.

If you are a monitor or coach going into programs to improve quality, your time is most likely focused on using a rating scale to assess how the teachers are measuring up to professional standards. You may spend much of your time meeting with the site director and going over scores, when you could be helping them think through ways the assessment tool can support teacher learning and what systems of support are needed for ongoing teacher reflection.

Although there may be benefits in all of these strategies, they typically address what teachers ought to know rather than *how* teachers learn. These approaches don't acknowledge that working with children is a complex, dynamic process that requires time and a focus to construct new understandings and best practices.

Right now, professional development in the early childhood field seems to be dominated by short, fragmented, one-shot workshops on a variety of topics, delivered by experts who offer strategies and techniques outside the context of daily teaching and learning with children. We call this approach *drive-through professional learning*. Like going through the window at a fast food restaurant, it is a convenient, familiar, economical way to meet requirements in a busy, fast-paced world (Carter 2010).

Whether we're talking about food or professional learning, there's no denying the appeal of quick-fix solutions when time and resources are limited. But deep down, we believe that we sell ourselves short when we rely on drive-through services to nourish ourselves as early childhood professionals. If we are going to thrive and grow, we clearly need something different.

A model for reflective teaching offers just that—something different.

A Reflective Model

We present four components to a model for supporting reflective early childhood teaching. Each one of these components addresses something many early childhood educators are longing for in their professional learning:

- time for focused dialogue
- communities of practice
- facilitators and critical friends
- reflective protocols

The value of each of these components is well-grounded in theory and research. Whatever your position in early childhood education, this workbook strives to bring each of the components of reflective practice to life in a practical way, one you can use in your day-to-day work.

Time for Focused Dialogue

In the early childhood work environment, time is precious. Teachers and administrators rarely have time to sit and reflect on their work, alone or with colleagues. When time is set aside for professional development, educators often feel pressure to cover many topics in a short period of time with no real depth of focus. In the reflective model, time for thoughtful study and dialogue is moved to the top of the to-do list. Whether setting aside ten minutes of planning time or an hour a week over the course of a year, educators who commit to focused reflection experience immediate and long-term benefits. Rather than focusing only on rules, problems, and complaints, teachers become more excited and engaged in their work, more enthusiastic and thoughtful about the materials and experiences they offer, and more focused on and delighted by the children's learning.

Communities of Practice

Although it is possible to be a reflective teacher on your own, reflecting with a group of coworkers offers a richer experience of camaraderie, multiple perspectives, deeper learning, and shared enjoyment of your work together. Early childhood administrators, consultants, and coaches can create support systems to make this possible for teachers.

The term *communities of practice* was first introduced in the work of Jean Lave and Etienne Wenger (1991). A community of practice is a group of people who share a concern or a passion for something they do and learn how to do it better as they interact regularly over time (Wenger, McDermott, and Snyder 2002).

Pause and Reflect

Consider Wenger's description of a community of practice.

Think of an informal community of practice you've been involved in. What was it like?

_____

_____

_____

How would you describe the benefits for yourself and others in the group?

_____

_____

_____

Each of us four authors has worked as an early childhood educator. We have always found ourselves drawn to others in our workplaces who want to talk about their day-to-day work with children. During our breaks and in the staff lounge, we eagerly began to discuss something interesting, curious, or confusing that a child or a group of children had done. We avoided conversations that focused on complaining or blaming children, families, or other staff members for our struggles. Instead, we shared a genuine sense of learning with each other. Though we couldn't always resist thinking there was a right answer, sometimes we resisted the urge to try to solve problems or find fault and instead thought about the *why* behind our collective wonderings.

In our discussions with coworkers, we loved trying to see things through the children's eyes. We considered possible things to add to the environment. Would they support or limit the play? The excitement at times was palpable! Often we had to cut the conversation short to get back to our rooms before each of us had gotten to fully say what we were thinking. It was frustrating not to be able to continue with the excitement of our conversation. At the end of the day, we sometimes found ourselves catching up with what happened in the parking lot before leaving for home. On the occasions when we got together socially after work, our conversations always circled back to the children. Through these interactions, we began to recognize the importance of making time to talk.

This kind of time with fellow educators gave us a way to focus on our work over time. We felt that problems didn't have to be solved right away—we had this group of people to come back to again and again. We could always count on someone to share a different perspective, to make us think more deeply about the *why* behind the decisions we made. Invariably in our discussions, someone was watching the clock and trying to make sure we all had a turn while supporting our reflective thinking and steering us away from fault finding. In effect, we had established an informal community of practice.

Whether informal or more carefully planned, communities of practice have been proven to be a powerful force for professional learning and growth in a variety of work environments. Regardless of the setting, positive change is more likely to happen and be sustained in moments when people doing the same work engage together over time with what Alma Fleet and Catherine Patterson (2001) describe as "waves of related ideas."

Facilitators and Critical Friends

When Margie asked her grandson Coe, at age five, what advice he would give teachers about how to get better at their job, he said, "Tell them to find someone to talk to. It's really lonely being a teacher." Children's perspectives can provoke deeper reflections for us.

Pause and Reflect

What do you think Coe might have seen or experienced in his preschool and kindergarten years that gave him this understanding?

_____

_____

_____

What might he notice if he watched *you* at work?

_____

_____

_____

It's true, early childhood teaching can be lonely work—even when you are surrounded by colleagues and children. Because you are working with active, constantly changing, living, breathing, squirming human beings, the job is often puzzling, never complete, and frequently overwhelming. That can leave you with a feeling of isolation and longing for someone who understands.

Wendy recalls the powerful impact that her mentor and supervisor Susan had on her life. As a young teacher, Wendy was excited and enthusiastic but full of questions and insecurities. Susan offered support by listening and asking thoughtful questions that helped Wendy find her own answers. Susan rarely told Wendy what to do. Instead, she supported her in uncovering her own ideas and thinking. Susan facilitated Wendy's learning and was an essential (or critical) friend to her.

Pause and Reflect

Think about someone who was or is essential to your learning.

Are you fortunate enough to have a Susan in your life? If so, who is it?

_____

How has someone been essential to something you have tried to learn?

_____

_____

_____

We believe that communities of practice are most responsive and successful when someone transparently steps into the role of the facilitator and critical friend. We see these two roles as similar but distinct in some important ways.

Being a Facilitator

The role of the facilitator is primarily to keep the group process moving forward with the task at hand. Facilitators give individual attention to group members, monitor group dynamics, offer clarification on issues or confusions, point out breakthroughs in understanding, and periodically summarize the ideas generated so far.

In our view, facilitators are a part of the community of practice. They keep the group focused and invite participants to add their ideas or perspectives. They point out connections between people's ideas. Facilitators can also contribute stories and examples related to the topic, but they should not try to be the group's *teachers* or dominate discussions. Stories facilitators offer should serve as a way to keep participants connected to the idea under discussion.

Being a Critical Friend

The role of a critical friend is slightly different from that of a facilitator. The word *critical* here is not used as meaning "to criticize" but rather to be essential and provocative for someone's learning (like critical thinking).

One of the most widely used definitions of a critical friend comes from the work of Arthur L. Costa and Bena Kallick (1993, 50), who describe a critical friend as "a trusted person who asks provocative questions, provides data to be examined through another lens, and offers critique of a person's work as a friend.... Critical friendships, therefore, must begin through building trust."

We see the role of a critical friend as indispensable to meaningful, focused learning in a community of practice. This role can be played by a facilitator but can also be played by any participant in the community. A critical friend consciously works to bring out the knowledge of the participants or thoughtfully encourages members of the community to explore their knowledge of theory, research, and best practice in order to deepen the understanding of the topic at hand. The critical friend is always listening for new knowledge that can be gained from a participant's contribution.

In a community of practice, a critical friend questions, provokes, brings forth different perspectives, and helps participants consider opportunities and possibilities for improving their practice. Critical friends may scaffold some new learning that the person couldn't quite get to without some kind of boost. Critical friends challenge others to see themselves as researchers in the teaching and learning process. All of this is done in a dance of challenge and support, so that both critical thinking and friendship are always present at the table.

Reflective Protocols

A protocol is a set of rules and procedures controlling an activity. Most early childhood professionals are familiar with protocols for diapering, hand washing, and cleaning tables. These protocols are tools for helping teachers organize health and safety activities. In a similar way, a reflective protocol is a tool for helping teachers organize their thinking about the complexity of the teaching and learning process.

In our work, we use a reflective protocol we call the Thinking Lens™. The Thinking Lens is a set of categories with questions that early childhood teachers can ask themselves when they consider something that is occurring in the moment or after the fact. The Thinking Lens categories and questions are given on pages 22–23. After some disciplined practice with the Thinking Lens, teachers learn the kinds of questions that help them make considered decisions for actions to take.

We've found the Thinking Lens to be particularly helpful to teachers who are reflecting together in a community of practice. Have you ever been part of professional group discussions that drifted off track before long? Perhaps people started griping or straying into other topics, and before long, time slipped away with no new insights uncovered. With time so limited and precious for professional discussions, we need to be more disciplined about our community of practice work. According to Joseph P. McDonald and his fellow researchers, "The kind of talking needed to educate ourselves cannot arise spontaneously and unaided from *just* talking. It needs to be carefully planned and scaffolded" (McDonald et al. 2003, 4). Reflective protocols support the development of that discipline.

Using a reflective protocol like the Thinking Lens offers other benefits to teachers working in communities of practice. As group members practice with the Thinking Lens questions over time, they start to develop a common language for their work together. This helps build relationships and make conversations easier. Using the Thinking Lens categories to open up new angles on the topic at hand, group members can enrich their discussions beyond the comfortable and familiar.

Above all, early childhood professionals who practice using a reflective protocol will, over time, develop an ongoing schema for making meaning of the continued complexity of their work. They learn to tap into three fields of knowledge that can help them become better at their work:

1.   The substantial knowledge they already bring to their work as practitioners

2.   The great body of public knowledge from theory, research, and best practices in our field

3.   The creative, innovative, unique knowledge that can be created from their collaborative work in a community of practice (Carter, Cotton, and Hill 2006)

In essence, communities of practice learn how to learn from, with, and on behalf of each other as early childhood professionals.

With ongoing participation in a community of practice with critical friends, you develop a new way of understanding professional development. Sandra Miller and Sonya Shoptaugh (2004, 248) describe the experience this way:

To enter into a style of teaching which is based on questioning what we're doing and why, on listening to children, on thinking about how theory is translated into practice and how practice informs theory, is to enter into a way of working where professional development takes place day after day in the classroom.

A Thinking Lens for Reflection and Inquiry

Use these Thinking Lens questions to help guide your thinking and discussions.

Knowing Yourself

- What captures my attention when the children engage, explore, and interact?
- What delights me as I watch and listen?
- What in my background and values is influencing my response to this situation and why?
- What adult perspectives—for example, standards, health and safety, time, and goals—are on my mind?

Finding the Details of Children's Competency That Engage Your Heart and Mind

- What do I notice in the children's faces and actions?
- Where do I see examples of children's strengths and competencies?
- What do I think is valuable about this experience?

Seeking the Child's Point of View

- What is the child drawn to and excited about?
- What might the child be trying to accomplish?
- Why might the child be interacting with others this way?
- What developmental themes, schemas, ideas, or theories might the child be exploring?

Examining the Physical/Social/Emotional Environment

- How is the organization and use of the physical space and materials impacting this situation?
- How could we strengthen relationships here?
- How are schedules and routines influencing this experience?

Considering Multiple Perspectives

- How might the child's culture and family background be influencing this situation?

- What questions might we ask to get the perspective of the child's family?

- Who else or what other perspectives should we consider?

- What child development or early learning theories should we consider in this experience?

- What desired early learning outcomes do I see reflected here?

Considering Opportunities and Possibilities for Next Steps

- What values, philosophy, and desired outcomes do I want to influence my response?

- What new or existing relationships could be strengthened?

- Which learning goals could be focused on here?

- What other materials and activities could be offered to build on this experience?

- What new vocabulary could we begin to use?

Adapted from *Learning Together with Young Children: A Curriculum Framework for Reflective Teachers* by Deb Curtis and Margie Carter, © 2008. Published by Redleaf Press, www.redleafpress.org.

How Facilitators/Critical Friends Can Support Reflection

- Make an effort to include all voices, notice who hasn't spoken, and invite contribution, without putting people on the spot.

- Help keep the group focused on the topic:

    "I'd like to call us back to this notion about _____."

    "I'm going to refocus us on the ideas we're exploring . . ."

- Invite people to add different ideas or perspectives:

    "I'm curious to hear if other folks have experienced that."

    "Is that true for all of you?"

    "Does someone have a different understanding?"

    "I wonder if there are other ways to think about that."

- Point out themes and connections between people's ideas or to the larger ideas being explored:

    "Your story underlines for me the idea that _____."

    "You're reminding us about _____."

    "How does this help you understand _____?"

- Restate a person's idea in a different form, referring to the big ideas the group is talking about together:

    "That sounds like you're saying _____."

    "Let me try to summarize your idea. I think you are talking about _____."

- Help people become aware of their own thinking and feelings:

    "What comes up for you as you sit with this idea?"

    "How does this fit with your experiences and understandings?"

    "Is anything making you squirm?"

- Allow silence! It takes time for people to gather their thoughts, to recall experiences, to frame their responses.

- Offer questions to the whole group for consideration. Or you might revisit an idea offered earlier in the conversation by another person in the group to help answer the question.

- Help bring new perspectives out in a group that reaches consensus quickly:

    "What perspective are we missing here?"

    "What aren't we saying?"

    "How would we explain this to someone who disagrees with us?"

CHAPTER 3

Getting Started

As you take on the challenge of launching a community of practice for reflective teaching, think about your own learning process. Consider how you typically like to learn about a new concept in your work:

- Do you take time by yourself to read, observe, and reflect on the concept?

- Do you discuss the concept with a trusted colleague who shares many of your beliefs?

- Do you try out the idea in practice to see how it works?

- Do you gather different perspectives by talking with others who don't necessarily share your beliefs?

Your initial response to this exercise may have been to answer, "All of the above!" Most of us use a combination of these learning approaches in our daily work, adapting ourselves to different learning situations as needed. Push yourself to think a little more deeply. Jot down your response to these questions: Which one of these approaches is your go-to style, the way you feel most comfortable and confident taking on a learning challenge? Why does that approach seem to work best for you?

_____

_____

_____

_____

_____

_____

One of the powerful elements of a community of practice model is that it can support individuals who may have very different approaches to learning. Teachers can study readings together, ground themselves in shared values, engage in and reflect on hands-on learning experiences, and challenge themselves with new ideas. Members of a community of practice make ongoing decisions about the most effective ways to learn together. To do this well, they need to take time to think about the *process* of learning in a group. They must continuously strive to understand themselves and others in the community as learners.

Pause and Reflect

Do some reflective writing or talk with a friend or colleague(s) to uncover more about yourself as a learner in a group. Use these questions to spark your thinking:

1. What intrigues you most about the idea of reflecting and learning together with a group of colleagues?

    _____

    _____

2. What would an ideal community of practice look or feel like to you? How would members work together?

    _____

    _____

3. What do you have to contribute to a group of colleagues learning together in a community of practice? What would you hope to gain from a community of practice?

    _____

    _____

4. Who do you have around you that might be interested in joining a community of practice? What common work interests do you share?

_____

_____

5. What resources and supports for this work do you have?

_____

_____

Asking yourself these kinds of questions will help you establish a vision for the work of your community of practice. This groundwork will help clarify your personal hopes and dreams for the learning opportunities and possibilities that lie ahead of you. There are a variety of ways to structure a community of practice to help the group reflect and gain new understanding together. No matter how you end up designing your community of practice, it is important for all members to feel that their learning needs are respected—that they have a unique voice that matters and would be missed if it wasn't included in the group.

Planting the Seed

Every community of practice has its own unique story of growth. Some spring up overnight; others need years to take root. Some grow organically; others are carefully planned and crafted. Some thrive with little feeding and maintenance; others require the ongoing care of a diligent gardener. Regardless of how they grow, all successful communities of practice seem to have one thing in common: along the way, at least one person decided the group was valuable, planted the seed, and committed to taking leadership to keep it going.

If you're reading this workbook, chances are pretty good that you're a person who would make that kind of commitment. Whether you're a teacher or family child care provider, a director, an administrator, or a teacher educator, think about the people who would be likely candidates to form a community of practice in your context. Who would be interested in and excited about this idea? Can you identify colleagues who may already informally gather to reflect together? Who are the key players you need to have on board?

Ideally, you will find others nearby who already share your passion for observing and studying children's learning. You may also be in the position to establish communities of practice to help others find and nurture that passion.

Considerations for Structuring Your Community

There's no single, simple magical recipe for creating an effective community of practice, but as you think about establishing your group, you might consider the following:

- diverse versus shared
- mandated versus voluntary
- structured versus flexible

Diverse versus Shared

One of the benefits of being part of a community of practice is being able to gain fresh perspectives from colleagues with differing points of view. We strongly believe that engaging in dialogue across diverse cultural, educational, experiential, dispositional, and professional backgrounds is not only valuable but also at the very heart of education for democracy. At the same time, every member of the community must feel enough trust and comfort with others in the group to take risks and fully participate. These feelings usually develop from commonly held beliefs, values, and interests.

Effective communities of practice balance members' diversity with a sense of shared purpose. Although this can be a fine line to walk, it usually helps to discuss this desired balance openly right from the start. When group members recognize the importance of both dissonance and agreement in group learning, they are more likely to establish a learning environment that supports both of these goals.

Mandated versus Voluntary

If you play a supervisory role in your setting, you will need to make a decision about whether or not to mandate participation in the community of practice model. You may have some compelling arguments for mandating participation.

Mandates send a strong message about organizational values and culture and create clear expectations for staff. Full staff participation in the communities of practice model can generate a powerful force for making lasting programmatic change. Alma Fleet and Catherine Patterson (2001, 1) describe this force as springing from a "critical mass" of teachers "all confronting and exploring similar aspects of their work together over time."

On the other hand, mandating participation in a community of practice is problematic in some obvious ways. It is pretty difficult to fire up any energy for deep reflection when group members are resistant or defiant. Put simply, you just can't force someone to reflect. Beyond that, by compelling teachers to participate in professional development that isn't related to a regulation requirement, you risk alienating them by not offering a choice of professional development that reflects their own interest. We believe in offering professional learning experiences that nourish teachers' hearts while challenging their thinking—difficult things to accomplish when teachers are mandated to be at the table.

We have seen many administrators successfully work through the decision to mandate or not to mandate by clarifying and articulating their program's goals and values for teachers' professional learning. This may require weighing individual teachers' needs against collective program needs. Again, transparency from the outset helps. When all involved are clear on the vision and potential benefits of the model, as well as the expectations for participation, we find that the vast majority of teachers are willing to enter into community of practice work with open minds and hearts.

Structured versus Flexible

One of the ongoing challenges for any community of practice is the tension between structure and flexibility. Structured groups value efficiency, adherence to planned agendas, and protocols to manage time and maximize productivity. Flexible groups are open ended, willing to go off the agenda, and value the collaboration process over specific learning outcomes. There are always trade-offs in balancing structure with flexibility. Choose structure, and you may sacrifice the responsiveness of creative, spontaneous, unrestricted dialogue. Opt for flexibility, and your group risks compromising its focus, losing track of time, and pursuing individual needs and interests instead of group learning.

Every community of practice has to develop its own harmony between flexibility and structure. Decisions about group processes should be made as consciously as possible, keeping the vision and goals of the community of practice in mind. And although it certainly helps to establish a sense of the group's style right from the start, most communities of practice clarify and adapt their processes as they change and grow over time. As Etienne Wenger (1998, 97) writes, "Learning involves a close interaction of order and chaos."

Examples of Community of Practice Structures

There are many communities of practice to be found in early childhood education. We've put together a list of some of the programs we are familiar with and how they function.

- **Hilltop Children's Center** is a nonprofit child care center in Seattle, Washington, with six classrooms. Over the last ten years the center has steadily shifted its budget and staffing patterns to allow each teaching team to meet once a week for ninety minutes and use a protocol of asking questions and reflecting to study the center's documentation. Teachers are expected to come to their weekly reflective meetings with an observation for the group to study and discuss. A mentor teacher serves as a facilitator/critical friend in these meetings, but the teachers have internalized the protocol so well that they can easily reflect on their own. As with the Thinking Lens protocol, participants always leave with a plan for taking some action. Once a month, the whole staff meets for professional development. During this time, they often work in communities of practice across their teaching teams, with a particular focus on developing their critical thinking. They take care to orient each new teacher who joins the staff into their reflective teaching practices and use of protocols.

- **The United Way Bright Beginnings** program in Houston, Texas, supports a cohort of site directors and three cohort groups made up of teachers working in infant, toddler, and preschool programs that serve low-income families. Working as communities of practice, the cohorts meet quarterly for an entire day, visiting each other's classrooms. Each cohort group offers children a collection of interesting, open-ended materials. Teachers initially explore the materials to learn more about their properties and possibilities and the vocabulary to use with them. Then the teachers go into one of their classrooms and offer these same materials for the children to explore. Teachers observe, take photos, and make notes to document the children's engagement. After the observations, the teachers meet together for the afternoon, using the Thinking Lens protocol to study their documentation and deepen their understanding of children and child development theory. Before leaving for the day, they work together to write a learning story describing one of the meaningful experiences they observed and its significance for the children's and their own learning. Cohort members return to their centers to share what they learn each time they meet as a community of practice.

- **Sound Child Care Solutions (SCCS)** is a consortium of seven to ten centers in Seattle, Washington, that have joined together to share some of their essential services through a central office. This frees up the site directors to focus less on running a business and more on the people in their programs. As part of its shared professional development services, SCCS sets up a community of practice group with the goal of developing more pedagogical leaders for the organization as a whole. Interested teachers fill out a short application form stating how they view their growing leadership and why they want to be part of the group. Selected teachers are then given release time by their site directors to come to a monthly meeting, where they are guided by a facilitator/critical friend to follow a similar process of exploring materials, observing and analyzing documentation, and then scheduling visits to each others' centers to practice the process with children. They learn to write learning stories and share these in the communities of practice meetings.

- **Montgomery Child Care Association** in Montgomery County, Maryland, offers a voluntary monthly curriculum work group to the staff at its nine child care programs. Teachers come together and form small group communities of six to eight participants, with an administrator facilitating each group. Facilitators guide the communities in using the Thinking Lens protocol to study observations and work samples of the children in their classrooms, using these observations to support ongoing curriculum planning and assessment.

- **Paradise Valley Community College** in Phoenix, Arizona, launched a community of practice project with an adjunct faculty member serving as the facilitator/critical friend. It offers an initial three-session class in which practicing teachers learn a process for reflective teaching, including using the Thinking Lens protocol, exploring engaging materials, and writing learning stories. This class is followed by a site visit to observe side-by-side modeling of using this process with children in six infant, toddler, and preschool classrooms. Teachers completing the class and site visit can then apply to be part of an ongoing community of practice under the guidance of the adjunct faculty member who serves as facilitator/critical friend. Membership entitles teachers to periodic side-by-side mentoring from the critical friend, who brings interesting materials to children, guides the observations and reflection processes, and supports collaborative writing of learning stories. The community of practice comes together across centers every six weeks to participate in a dialogue about reflective teaching and the ideas in its course book, *Learning Together with Young Children: A Curriculum Framework for Reflective Teachers* by Deb Curtis and Margie Carter.

- At **Harvest Resources Associates**, we offer Reflective Practices Institutes that bring together a hundred or so participants to focus deeply on a topic for two to three days in a community of practice model. Small groups of six to eight participants stay together and work with a facilitator throughout all sessions of the institute. Presentations by a leader are followed by facilitated small-group sessions that explore questions and undertake activities that apply the ideas from the presentation. Facilitators meet before and during the institute to discuss the institute's content as well as the group process and to practice becoming critical friends for the participants in their groups. A list of currently scheduled Reflective Practices Institutes can be found on the Harvest Resources Associates website at www.ecetrainers.com.

Pause and Reflect

Think about how you might want to set up a community of practice.

1. Which of the examples we've described helps you think about possibilities for your own work setting?

   _____

2. If you were to adapt one of these examples for your own work setting, where would you start? What would be your first step?

   _____

   _____

   _____

3. Who might you involve to help you develop and lead a model of reflection for your community of practice?

   _____

From Group to Community

Once you have potential group members and a structure for your community in mind, it is important to engage all community members in an honest discussion about group learning. One way to start this discussion is by sharing stories about group learning experiences. Here are some potential discussion starters:

- Describe a group learning experience that inspired or invigorated you.

- Describe a time when you helped a group overcome a barrier.

- Describe how you want this group to look, sound, and feel at some projected point in the future.

- Describe some things that help you learn in a group.

After listening to each other's stories, reflect alone or individually to identify some of the strengths that group members bring to the community. Also consider some of the potential challenges that lie ahead of you.

We've found that the biggest hurdle facing early childhood professionals in establishing communities of practice is developing enough trust to share the good, the bad, and the ugly of their teaching experiences with each other. Ironically, this kind of trust may be hardest to develop among professionals who care deeply about their work. It takes a lot of courage to speak openly about all the passion, fear, joy, sorrow, excitement, frustration, and confusion that can arise from working with young children (and that's just in one day's work!). But Parker J. Palmer (2007a, 148) reminds us of the following:

> The growth of any craft depends on shared practice and honest dialogue among the people who do it. We grow by private trial and error, to be sure— but our willingness to try, and fail, as individuals is severely limited when we are not supported by a community that encourages such risks.

One way that members of a community of practice can support each other in taking these risks is by deeply listening to one another.

Stopping in the Middle to Listen

In the classic children's book *Owl at Home* (Lobel 1975), we find poor Owl worrying about his upstairs when he is downstairs, and his downstairs when he is upstairs. He runs frantically up and down the stairs over and over again, frustrating and exhausting himself, trying desperately to keep watch over his whole house. Finally, he plops himself down in the middle of the stairs, realizing that he just can't be in two places at once.

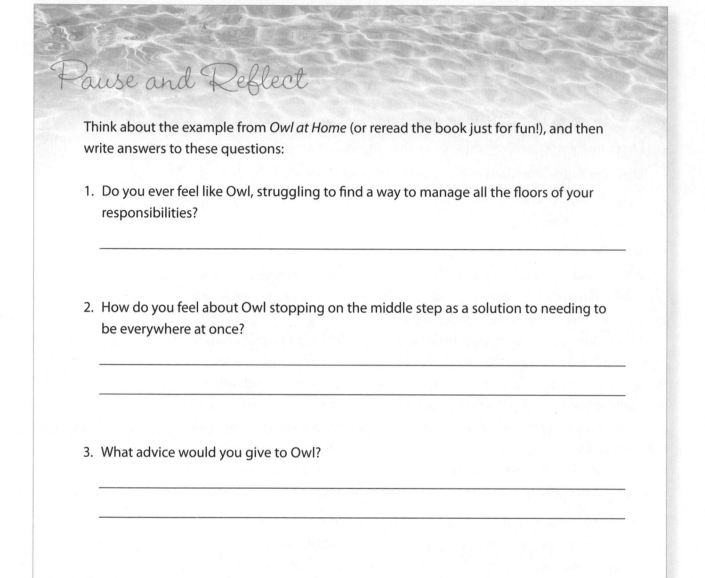

Pause and Reflect

Think about the example from *Owl at Home* (or reread the book just for fun!), and then write answers to these questions:

1. Do you ever feel like Owl, struggling to find a way to manage all the floors of your responsibilities?

   _____

2. How do you feel about Owl stopping on the middle step as a solution to needing to be everywhere at once?

   _____

   _____

3. What advice would you give to Owl?

   _____

   _____

We find that many early childhood professionals relate to Owl's dilemma because they must oversee multiple personal and professional commitments with the best intent of doing it all. This kind of frenzied pace makes professional reflection nearly impossible.

Even if it seems impossible to slow down the pace of your busy lives, your community of practice can make a conscious choice to establish a place in the middle of the stairs for deep listening. This kind of listening is more than just listening politely, even more than actively listening. Deep listening is listening on the edge of your seat, paying close attention to the deeper meaning and intent behind the words of the speaker. When you listen deeply, you are try-ing to understand who someone *is*, not just understanding what the speaker says. Author Brenda Ueland (1993, 205–6) describes the power of this kind of listening:

> Listening is a magnetic and strange thing, a creative force. . . . When we are listened to, it creates us, makes us unfold and expand. Ideas actually begin to grow within us and come to life. . . . When we listen to people there is an alternating current, and this recharges us so that we never get tired of each other. . . . This little creative fountain inside us begins to spring and cast up new thoughts and unexpected laughter and wisdom. . . . It is when people really listen to us, with quiet, fascinated attention, that the little fountain begins to work again, to accelerate in the most surprising way.

Pause and Reflect

Think about a time when you felt someone really listened to you.

1. Briefly describe the situation. When and where did it happen? Who was there? What were you talking about?

   _____

   _____

   _____

   _____

2. How would you describe the feelings you experienced?

   _____

   _____

   _____

Deep listening is a skill that can be practiced and learned. Your community of practice may want to set aside time to build your skills at deep listening, particularly if you find yourselves feeling like Owl, overwhelmed and out of breath when you come into your meeting time together. Some groups find the following exercise worthwhile:

- Set a time period for each speaker (no fewer than two minutes).

- Offer an open-ended story starter: What's on your mind?

- As the speaker shares, the listeners focus on deep listening—clearing their minds and agendas; staying silent; avoiding paraphrasing, interrupting, or offering advice. The goal is to be in the moment with the speaker and to create a safe and supportive atmosphere for your work together.

Setting Agreements

Setting agreements for group processes is another key element in establishing trust and productive reflection among members. Agreements help establish expectations for group participation and remind members to consider others' learning needs. Agreements help curb unproductive behaviors and serve as a grounding place if discussions get heated. Your agreements set the tone for your community's collaborative culture.

There are many ways to go about setting agreements. Members can simply list behaviors that support or challenge group learning and then work together to draw agreements from those lists. Alternatively, members can write suggestions for agreements on index cards and compile them on a master list. If less time is available, a facilitator can offer a list of possible group agreements, and group members can add suggestions that modify the list to meet their needs. No matter how you develop your agreements, we suggest keeping the list short, focused on essentials, and stated as commitments to act or behave in certain ways rather than as more general beliefs. For instance, rather than just saying, "We will show each other respect," add what respect might look like: "We will show each other respect by listening thoughtfully and not interrupting." These common issues are addressed in most agreements:

- What are your community's expectations about presence and participation?

- What are your community's expectations about time and agendas?

- How does your community expect members to share the airspace so that all voices are heard and no voices dominate?

- How will your community maintain its focus on the discussion at hand?

- How will your community support diverse styles of learning?

- How do you expect members to respond to differing perspectives?

- What are your community's expectations for handling conflict?

- What are your community's expectations for the facilitator (if you have one)?

- How will community members be critical friends to each other and help deepen each other's learning?

When your community comes to consensus on a set of agreements, we encourage you to take the time to make a commitment to each other to honor those agreements. This act lends some weight to the work you've already done together and to the journey you're about to undertake together.

These agreements aren't rules set permanently in stone. They can—and should—be revisited over time. Are your agreements serving you well? Are members upholding them? Are any changes needed? Used with such considerations in mind, your community agreements become a way of "re-membering" your shared vision and commitment to your community of practice.

A Reflective Community of Practice at Work

Here is an example of a group of reflective early childhood professionals engaging in community of practice work together. Kimberly is a program director who meets regularly with teachers Ana, Sasha, and Greg. Kimberly serves as the facilitator for their discussions. She leads off this discussion by sharing a photo observation from a recent classroom visit.

Ryan and the Rain

Three-year-old Ryan frowned when his teacher said the sky was getting dark and it looked like rain. He said in a low, steady voice, "I don't want it to get dark. I don't want it to rain." His teacher heard him and responded, "But rain will make the flowers grow." Ryan stayed firm in his position: "I don't want the flowers to grow. I don't want the grass to grow." Ryan ran to the closest window, which was well above his eye level. Stepping into a nearby doll bed, he moved up closer to the window ledge. After slipping a bit, he stepped back down. Finally, he slid a nearby chair over to the window and climbed up on it. Now Ryan had a clear view of the outside. He stood nearly still on the chair for half a minute, eyes focused outside the window. With a crinkled nose and squinting his eyes, he said, "I want to hold that rain."

Discussion	Comments
Kimberly: I observed this situation with Ryan last week and I thought it raised some interesting points we could talk about in our first ten minutes together.	*Facilitator gathers and focuses the group, setting a time limit for the discussion.*
Can we start with a round-robin read of the scenario?	*In a round-robin read, members take turns reading a sentence or two of the scenario aloud. This technique is helpful for auditory learners and can support group process by getting all voices involved in the discussion from the start.*
[*Group members take turns reading sentences from the observation.*]	
Kimberly: And before we go on, will someone volunteer to read what they see in the photo?	*Reading the photo is a great role for keen observers and helps others learn to look for the details.*
Greg: Sure—this looks like a photo of Ryan looking out the window at the rain. He's got both feet solidly planted on a wooden chair and is probably three feet or so from the window. Another child seems to be playing in the area between Ryan and the window—possibly with the doll bed the observation mentioned. Ryan's arms are at an interesting angle from his sides—he almost looks ready to move.	
Kimberly: Thanks, Greg. So let me put this out to anybody: What sparks your interest in Ryan and the rain?	*The Thinking Lens: Know Yourself*
Greg: Well, the first thing that catches my interest is him standing on the chair.	
Sasha: Right, that would catch my interest in the classroom too! My first instinct is safety—I'd probably want him to get down off the chair.	*There seems to be some shared interest in this topic.*
Kimberly: Let's think this through a little more together. Talk a little more about that, Sasha.	

Discussion	Comments
Sasha: I think we're trained as teachers to think "Safety first." We can't just let all the children climb on chairs—it would be chaos. And we don't want anyone getting hurt.	
Kimberly: So there's a value behind that reaction—can you name it, Sasha? How would you explain that to someone—why would you want him to get down from the chair?	*Kimberly asks questions as a critical friend to help Sasha name her values.*
Sasha: [*thinks for a moment*] Well, there are two reasons, I think. First, I value keeping children safe so they don't get hurt. Second, I guess I value a sense of order so all the kids don't follow Ryan and jump up on chairs.	*Sasha goes deeper here.*
Greg: But when you really look at the photo, neither of those things is happening. He really does seem to be sturdy on that chair. And the other child in the photo doesn't seem to be copying his behavior at all.	*Greg points out another way of looking at the situation.*
Kimberly: So you're seeing some of the details of Ryan's competence, Greg. Say more about that—what else do you notice about Ryan's skills and abilities in this observation?	*The Thinking Lens: Find the Details of the Competent Child*
Greg: Well, if you think about it, he's a really good problem solver. He was trying to get to the window, and he showed a lot of initiative in figuring out a way to do it.	
Sasha: That's true. And it's interesting—I wonder if he deliberately picked the wooden chair to stand on because it's sturdier and flatter than that red plastic chair beside him?	*Greg and Sasha are framing Ryan in a more competent light here.*

Discussion	Comments
Kimberly: I didn't notice that before, Sasha. That red chair might have been lighter and easier to move, so it really might have been a conscious decision on Ryan's part. That makes me think about other ways this physical environment is affecting his exploration. Let's pause for a minute and think about that. (pause)	*Even though she is facilitating, Kimberly is open to learning too.* *The Thinking Lens: Examine the Physical/Social/Emotional Environment* *Good to take a pause now and then—it takes time to reflect.*
Kimberly: Ana, we haven't heard from you yet. Any thoughts about the physical environment?	*Kimberly brings Ana into the discussion.*
Ana: I don't like the room arrangement.	
Greg: Can you be more specific on that?	*Greg helps deepen the learning with this question for Ana.*
Ana: Well, ideally, you want him to be able to see out that window, right? There wouldn't even be a problem with the chair if he could just see out the window. It looks like the window is low enough that he could see out if there wasn't all that stuff in front of it.	*Ana takes up Greg's challenge and gives specifics to back up her thinking.*
Greg: [*looking at picture again*] That's true.	
Sasha: I was thinking that too. It's great when the kids can get to the windows and see out. Our kids love to watch the rain. We usually go out in it too. Just get the parents to bring rain boots and umbrella, and you're good to go!	
Greg: You have to be careful about that, though, if parents don't all bring raingear.	*The conversation is starting to drift a little here.*
Kimberly: Let me pull us back to Ryan. Ana, you were saying that you would ideally want Ryan to be able to see out that window. Can you explain more about that? Why do you feel that would be a worthwhile experience for him to have?	*Kimberly acts as facilitator to refocus the group.* *Then she acts as a critical friend to help Ana go deeper.*

Discussion	Comments
Ana: [*pauses to think*] I guess because it seems so important to him. Something about the rain really seems to be on his mind.	
Kimberly: Yeah. I think so too. What about that? What do you think might be on his mind? What might he be thinking about or feeling?	*The Thinking Lens: Seek the Child's Perspective*
Sasha: I was wondering if he was scared. Maybe he's had some experience with a thunderstorm or something.	
Ana: Or maybe he just really thinks the rain is mysterious. Because he says he doesn't want it to rain, but then it sort of seems like he *does* want to watch it.	*This discussion could go a lot longer—teachers tend to get very engaged once they start seeking the child's perspective!*
Greg: I'd love to know more about his thinking. [*others nod*] That's the thing—if we just tell him to get down off the chair, we never find out.	
Kimberly: So that's a really complex decision for you to make as a teacher, right? You have these values of safety and order, and there's a place for those. Then there's this competing value of pursuing this interesting investigation that seems significant to this child.	*Kimberly acts as both a facilitator and a critical friend to summarize the discussion and offer a specific new provocation.*
How do you decide what you're going to do in the moment? What values would you want to drive your response to Ryan?	*The Thinking Lens: Consider Opportunities and Possibilities*
	At this point, the discussion could continue; it could end with some individual written reflection, or the questions could hang, to be picked up again at a later point.

CHAPTER 4

Using the Reflective Model in Different Settings

Making a Commitment to Reflection

Ideas about what it means to be a reflective early childhood professional abound in our field. Some people equate being reflective with a high level of individual experience or education, and some try to quantify it, using program quality standards or outcomes. We think of reflective teaching as a disposition—a mind-set for working with young children that is attainable to early childhood professionals at all levels of education and experience. But we agree with William Ayers (2004, 109–10), who says "reflection is more than thinking, although thinking and thoughtfulness are essential to begin."

Pause and Reflect

Reflection is a word that has many possible interpretations. After reading the first three chapters of this workbook, which of the following dictionary definitions of *reflection* most closely matches your impression of the word?

Reflection can mean

- a calm, lengthy consideration
- the phenomenon of an image being thrown back from a surface
- an expression without words
- a likeness in which left and right are reversed

Discuss your answer with a critical friend or with several others in your community of practice. What are the similarities and differences in the ways each of you interprets the idea of reflection? What does it mean *to you* to be a reflective teacher?

Cultivating a reflective disposition requires discipline, mindfulness, and a commitment to developing systems and structures to make meaning of your work and your role as a professional. Here are some stories about early childhood professionals who are making a commitment to reflective teaching practices in a variety of work settings.

Do You See Yourself in Any of These Stories?

Read through the following stories, and think about each situation. Ask yourself if you are like the person in the story. How is her experience similar to yours? How is her experience different?

Jo's Story

Family child care provider Jo is dedicated to her career, and she takes it seriously. She takes pride in offering a home-based program built on close, trusting relationships with children and families. Jo is always trying to learn and grow in her work, but she faces significant hurdles finding nourishing and challenging professional learning experiences in her community. Finding the time is always an issue, but so is finding providers who want to think together about their work. Every day, Jo stops to take notice of the magical moments unfolding among the children in her care. She spends time looking back over the photographs she's taken and writes out her thoughts in her journal when time allows. Although she shares her observations with the children and families, she longs for a forum in which she can study them at a deeper level with a caring colleague or two.

Jo can use this workbook as a support for defining herself as a reflective early childhood professional. She can use it to consider the value of reflection in her work and to commit herself to setting up a time and structure for reflecting on her observations in a more focused way, using the Thinking Lens protocol.

As Jo learns about the reflective model, she might consider reaching out to others to find a critical friend or to form a community of practice to support her ongoing professional learning. She can use ideas from this workbook to spark her thinking about how to find like-minded colleagues in her own community to build an online learning community.

IDEAS FOR FAMILY PROVIDERS

- Use this book to enhance your identity as a reflective professional.
- Practice using the Thinking Lens protocol as you study your observations of children.

- Encourage other family providers to join you in using the workbook.

- Encourage your local family child care association or R&R to host communities of practice based on the ideas in this book.

Lynne's Story

Lynne was an elementary school teacher for many years before she found her true calling—working with toddlers and two-year-olds in a child care program. She considers herself a newbie to the early childhood field, and she has found true joy and inspiration learning with these very young children. She wants nothing more than to share her enthusiasm with the other teachers in her team. Lynne and her colleagues are given an hour of paid planning time every week, but that never seems to be enough to get into meaty discussions about the children unless there is a problem at hand. Lynne finds herself frustrated by these meetings and yearns for some time when she and her team can focus on the wonders and competencies of the children instead of problems, logistics, and deficits.

Lynne can use this workbook to continue articulating what she believes about herself as a reflective teacher. She can thoughtfully consider and advocate for an expanded vision of team planning in her program. She can use this book to validate her beliefs about the importance of reflection, explain her beliefs to her team members and director, and rally support for more professional learning opportunities that support reflective teaching.

Working together, Lynne and her colleagues can choose to use the hour of planning time they have in a much more thoughtful way. They can work as a community of practice, using components of the reflective model to structure their meetings, and setting aside time for reflection on specific activities from the study sessions.

IDEAS FOR TEACHERS

- Continue to study this workbook and other resources such as *Learning Together with Young Children: A Curriculum Framework for Reflective Teachers* and the second edition of *The Art of Awareness: How Observation Can Transform Your Teaching*, both by Deb Curtis and Margie Carter, so that you can confidently speak about reflective teaching.

- Encourage your teaching team to start using the study sessions in this book as a way to launch your work together as a community of practice.

- Keep a copy of the Thinking Lens protocol handy, and during the day practice asking yourself questions under each of the areas for reflection so that this process becomes second nature to how you work.

- Practice studying your observations and writing documentation stories using Thinking Lens protocol with your teaching team.

- Ask your director for time during all staff meetings to share the new way you and your teaching team are working.

Courtney's Story

Courtney is a new director in a large preschool and school-age child care program. Before taking this position, she was a preschool teacher in an innovative program that put reflective, deeply child-centered teaching and learning at the center of the curriculum. She and her colleagues tuned in to the details of children's explorations and regularly engaged in reflective dialogue around their observations and documentation. Now that Courtney finds herself in a leadership position in a new program, she is determined to promote and support the value of reflective teaching practices. She knows that this will involve helping people change their thinking and current behavior, but she is committed to taking small, but significant, thoughtful steps toward her vision.

Courtney can use this workbook to revisit and recommit herself to the values of reflection and reflective teaching and supervision. As she strengthens and models her own beliefs, she puts herself in a better position to share her vision in ways that motivate and inspire others. Courtney can create a climate of excitement by encouraging her team to notice the remarkable things children do every day. As a director, she can begin to make shifts in her budget and staffing patterns to provide time for teaching teams to meet and reflect on what the children have been doing and how they might plan from that. She can use the Thinking Lens protocol and this book to establish ways for teachers to think and talk about how they see their work. As ripples of interest and enthusiasm pick up, Courtney can be ready to seek out individual teachers who are ready to take on the work, introduce them to the components of the reflective model, and get started on organizing team meetings as communities of practice using the Thinking Lens.

IDEAS FOR DIRECTORS, SITE MANAGERS, AND PROGRAM COORDINATORS

- Commit yourself to becoming a promoter of reflective, not just compliant, teaching.

- Reread this workbook to develop priorities and an action plan for yourself for how you want to promote reflective teaching in your center. Other valuable resources to inspire and help you in this planning process are the second edition of *The Visionary Director: A Handbook for Dreaming, Orga-*

nizing, and Improvising in Your Center by Margie Carter and Deb Curtis and the DVD *Right from the Start: A Guide to Hiring, Orienting, and Supporting Teachers for Reflective Practices* by the Hilltop Children's Center.

- Begin to regularly tell stories about the remarkable things you see children in your program doing. To create a culture of excitement about observing children, invite other teachers to do the same.

- Open your regular staff meetings by asking a teacher to volunteer a short story about something learned by watching children.

- Ask for volunteers to start meeting with you to plan how to use this workbook in your center. From this group, develop a leadership team that focuses on the workbook's guidelines on facilitation and being a critical friend.

- Create a strategic plan for how to begin shifting budget line items and staffing patterns so teachers can have weekly team meetings focused on reflecting and planning based on their observations of children.

- Bring these ideas to your local directors' group to generate interest and to help you find colleagues to think and plan with.

Franklin's Story

Franklin works for a large organization responsible for quality improvement in a variety of early childhood programs across his city. His role is to monitor for quality using a variety of assessment tools and to provide technical assistance with training and consultations in areas needing improvement. Franklin spends more time with teacher supervisors (education coordinators, site directors, program managers) than with teachers. He senses that teacher supervisors are often disconnected from the life of the classroom, overwhelmed by their responsibilities, and in many cases, not very happy in their jobs. He can use this book to gain ideas about how to focus his work on reflection more than compliance. Sharing the book with the site directors, supervisors, and coordinators, he can suggest they get together as a group to discuss how they see their roles and where some changes can be made to provide more opportunities for reflection. He can lobby to have his organization host communities of practice that staff from all the sites can be invited to, eventually using the practice sessions of this workbook.

IDEAS FOR QUALITY ENHANCEMENT PROJECT ADMINISTRATORS

- Become clear in your own thinking about the difference between focusing on compliance and reflective practice.

- Analyze your work practices to see what can be changed to promote more reflection.

- Create a vision statement that accurately reflects your hopes and dreams as a quality enhancement project administrator. What are the core values and beliefs that brought you to your work? How can you better align your current practice with those beliefs and values? Describe one key component of your vision statement that you plan to bring to life. Share this reflection with a critical friend.

- Introduce this workbook to site directors, education coordinators, and supervisors, individually and in a meeting where everyone can discuss it together.

- As you work with site directors, education coordinators, and supervisors, explore how they view the teachers they work with. Do they understand the difference between supervising and mentoring? What do they understand about how teachers learn? For more about images of teachers and teacher learning, read Margie Carter and Deb Curtis's *The Visionary Director: A Handbook for Dreaming, Organizing, and Improvising in Your Center*, second edition.

- Invite those you work with to reflect on this remark made by Thomas Merton (quoted in Palmer 2007b, 72): "We're called to give our hearts to the world, but first we have to have our hearts in our own possession. We cannot give to others what we ourselves don't possess." Is it possible that compliance tends to rob teachers of their own hearts? If so, how might we help teachers reclaim their hearts? Explore these ideas within your agency, and encourage others to consider hosting communities of practice as part of their quality enhancement work. Engage in some reflecting together on how to connect early learning standards or assessment results with the core values of the agency. Where within these standards or assessments are the places that you most want your agency to excel because they reflect your own values and vision?

Randall's Story

Randall spent many years as a preschool teacher and director before he became a trainer. Although he misses being in a program every day, he loves his work developing and conducting workshops, presenting keynotes, and consulting in classrooms. He is well known in his community for being able to deliver dry content in fun and interactive ways. He is a skilled storyteller, and using his humor and creativity, he can almost always get a group of teachers engaged. He loves sharing experiences from his own classroom teaching days with others and offering lots of helpful tips and techniques along the way.

But, despite the glowing evaluations he typically receives, Randall can't fight an underlying sense of disconnection in his work. Most of the training he is asked to do is delivered in short, fragmented two-to-three-hour sessions outside the context of teachers' day-to-day classroom experience. He has little opportunity to develop ongoing relationships with individual teachers, listen to *their* stories, and help them think through the complexity of their work.

Randall has spent his career advocating for teaching practices that support how children learn best. He can use this workbook to help ensure that his *own* teaching practices are now supporting how *teachers learn best.* He can begin by reviewing the elements of reflective teaching and reconsidering the components of a reflective model of professional development. As he does this, he can think about ways to better align his own work with this model. He can consider opportunities to use his time with teachers for more focused study and dialogue about the real experiences they face in their classrooms. Instead of offering teachers a host of techniques to try, he can introduce them to a protocol for thinking through their responses to children. He can learn more about the role of a critical friend and bring this role into his consulting work. He can think about ways of moving himself out of the role of the sage on the stage and establishing more communities of practice among teachers during his trainings.

IDEAS FOR TRAINERS

- Reflect on your ideas about teachers' learning and growth. Are you modeling teaching approaches with adult learners that parallel the approaches you hope they will take with young children? What images do you hold of the adult learners in your training sessions? Challenge yourself to see them as competent, capable, curious, classroom decision makers rather than as people who need to be filled with knowledge or fixed with tips and techniques.

- Review your course outlines carefully, and reflect on the opportunities you are providing for adult learners to construct their own knowledge. Are you creating many opportunities for people to share their individual experiences and understandings? How are you helping teachers to find and articulate their own voices and solve their own problems? How are you engaging teachers who have differing needs, interests, and learning styles?

- Learn more about the role of a facilitator/critical friend and consider ways in which you can take on this role in your trainings. Helpful resources might be *The Facilitator's Book of Questions: Tools for Looking Together at Student and Teacher Work* by David Allen and Tina Blythe, *Becoming a Critically Reflec-*

tive Teacher by Stephen D. Brookfield, and *Teaching with Your Mouth Shut* by Donald L. Finkel.

- Use this workbook to help develop a vision of effective professional learning that goes beyond fragmented, one-shot training sessions. Practice articulating the elements of your vision and the core values behind it. Become an advocate for the elements of the reflective model (time for focused study, communities of practice, critical friends/facilitators, and reflective protocols). Help your clients create professional development systems and structures that support these elements and teachers' ongoing reflection and learning.

Yanette's Story

Yanette can so clearly remember the excitement, anticipation, and nervousness she felt years ago when she started teaching preschool. All those feelings are now coming up again for her as she takes on the challenge of teaching a college course for preservice early childhood teachers.

As in her work teaching young children, Yanette feels an immense sense of responsibility for her adult students. She wants to set these prospective teachers up to succeed in their future work, but she has so little time to cover so much content. She wants her students to value social constructivist learning theory, and she wants to be a role model for them. In this age of teacher-proof curricula, how does she help these teachers begin to see themselves as confident, professional decision makers?

Yanette can use this workbook to remember and validate her own beliefs and experiences as a reflective teacher. She can give careful thought to the kinds of supports that reflective teachers need and deserve. She can work to align her course with the components of the reflective model, putting a greater emphasis on studying children, rather than focusing exclusively on the technical aspects of setting up activities for children or so-called methodology. In assignments and in-class discussions, she can provide her students with ongoing practice in collegial reflection and thoughtful decision making using a protocol like the Thinking Lens. When seeking approval for her courses, she can treat the identified learning outcomes as something to study with her students, investigating quality instead of only compliance.

Yanette knows that many potential barriers lie in front of her. She is working in a system with layer upon layer of accountability and bureaucracy. There are probably rules and regulations fighting against any change she might want to make. But she also knows that her students will face these same kinds of barriers in their own work. By keeping her vision and values at the forefront of her teaching practice, she can serve as a role model and mentor for them. As she thinks it through, she realizes that she may need her own critical friend or community of practice for support as she takes on this challenge. She immediately thinks of her dear friend and colleague Maria and realizes how long it has been since they talked. She's smiling as she picks up her phone.

IDEAS FOR COLLEGE INSTRUCTORS

- Revisit the ideas that underpin your work. Do you focus as much on *how* teachers learn as you do on *what* they need to know? Do you apply Lev Vygotsky's theory of co-constructing knowledge? Helpful resources include *Training Teachers: A Harvest of Theory and Practice* by Margie Carter and Deb Curtis, *In Search of Understanding: The Case for Constructivist Classrooms* by Jacqueline Grennon Brooks and Martin G. Brooks, and the third edition of *The Having of Wonderful Ideas: And Other Essays on Teaching and Learning* by Eleanor Duckworth.

- Revisit your course syllabi, and consider how to revamp their structure for more collaborative reflection on the ideas you are offering. Consider turning some of your assignments into mini-research projects using a protocol such as the Thinking Lens.

- To offer your students an opportunity to engage in reflective practice with other students in your college class, try activities like these:

  1. Ask students to choose an artifact from an early childhood classroom to share with the class. These could include a piece of child's artwork, a video of children working on a particular project, photographs of children at play, or portfolio documentation. The artifact should be something of interest to the students that they'd like to think more about and about which they'd like to gather insight and input from others.

  2. Set up small groups of four to five students. In round-robin fashion, have students take turns sharing their artifact. They can offer a brief description of the context of the artifact. In round-robin fashion, the other students can respond to the following questions about the artifact:

     - As you look at the artifact, what do you see?

     - What questions does the artifact raise for you?

     - What do you think the child (or children) is (are) working on or learning?

     - How does this artifact connect with your own ideas about teaching young children?

     - Any ideas on how the teacher in this classroom might extend this learning experience?

3. After all the students have had an opportunity to present their artifacts to the small group, reconvene as a whole group. Ask students to share feedback about what insights they gained from this process.

4. Offer an experience of studying an article together in a community of practice that uses a protocol honoring all perspectives and that creates the emotional safety to offer different points of view. The protocol can be as simple as this (McDonald et al. 2003):

    *   Have all the students speak for up to two minutes about a section of the article that had particular meaning for them. Each listener in turn has one uninterrupted minute to reflect back on what the presenter has said. Remember that reflecting back means exploring the presenter's interpretation of the passage, not adding one's own interpretation. For example, "From what you said, I can see that you are concerned about . . ." See chapter 2 of this workbook, "A Model to Support Reflective Teaching," for ideas. Allow the presenter a final minute to respond to what has been learned from the reflective feedback.

As you consider what excites you about the ideas in this workbook, make a plan to move your early childhood teaching toward more intentional, reflective practices that keep teachers and children learning in the classroom day after day.

Our thanks to colleagues Christie Colunga, Ann Hentschel, Kristie Norwood, Ijumaa Jordan, and Valerie Rajotte for sharing ideas and experiences from their programs to help us in writing this chapter.

Community of Practice Sessions

The study session activities on the following pages are meant to help you reflect on your work using the Thinking Lens protocol to heighten your self-awareness, strengthen your image of children, examine the details of your teaching and learning environment, and challenge yourself with new perspectives.

Keeping the elements of a reflective professional learning model in mind, we've organized the activities and exercises in these study sessions to fit with the realities of professional life in most busy early childhood programs. The sessions were developed for reflecting in communities of practice—small groups of four to eight early childhood colleagues who meet together over time. These ten study sessions offer opportunities for reflective collaboration and dialogue within the discipline of a protocol if your community meets regularly for one to two hours at a time. You can follow the sequential order of the study sessions offered here or pick and choose from among them.

Each study session is focused around a key concept of reflective teaching in early childhood settings. The sessions are designed to help you and your colleagues connect theory and best practices to the practical, day-to-day events that continuously unfold in your classrooms. Each session typically includes five sections, although not always in the same order:

- an opening activity to help you and your colleagues begin to identify what you already know or think about the topic

- a scenario to study together

- hands-on experiences to engage in

- a field study to take back into your classroom work

- resources for further exploration

In every session, we offer questions from the Thinking Lens protocol to help deepen your discussions and promote learning. Your group may want to select a facilitator/critical friend who will take on the role of focusing, guiding, and challenging the group's learning using the Thinking Lens questions. This can be one person who takes on this role for one or more study sessions or a participant chosen to take on the role for an individual activity or experience.

An important part of being a reflective professional is being aware of your own learning needs and interests. Toward that goal, we wholeheartedly encourage you to use these study sessions, to improvise, and to adapt them as you see fit. We also encourage you to practice using the disciplined protocol of the Thinking Lens to avoid drifting off into other discussions.

Each of the study sessions is designed for about two hours of community of practice work, depending on the depth of your discussions. The field studies will typically take a minimum of one hour of teachers' time between sessions. If time is a concern, you can break up the sessions and select activities or experiences that will work with the time you have available. Although we think reflective dialogue is most productive in small groups, you may need to structure the discussions for partners (dyads) so that you can work in smaller or larger groups. You can get creative by substituting observation scenarios or materials from your own program as needed.

However you choose to use these study sessions, we encourage you to approach them with openness, tolerance for ambiguity, imagination, and a strong image in mind of children, families, your colleagues, and yourself.

Examining Your Values

Identifying the values that influence your teaching practices is one of the most important professional development activities you can take up. Values influence everything you do, whether you have intentionally identified them or not. Your community of practice can help you clarify your values and examine how your environment, curriculum, and interactions reflect them.

Opening Activity

Read the following quotations.

> We want to know what the children think, feel, and wonder. We believe that the children will have things to tell each other and us that we have never heard before. We are always listening for a surprise and the birth of a new idea. This practice supports a . . . searching together for new meaning. Together, we become a community of seekers.—Louise Boyd Cadwell (2003, 25)

> The key is curiosity, and it is curiosity, not answers, that we model. As we seek to learn more about a child, we demonstrate the acts of observing, listening, questioning, and wondering. When we are curious about a child's words and our responses to those words, the child feels respected. The child *is* respected.—Vivian Gussin Paley (1986, 127)

> We are part of an ongoing story of men and women, ideals intact, who realize that history can be changed, and that it is changed by making it our own—starting with the future of children.—Loris Malaguzzi (2000, 14–15)

Our mission is to plant ourselves at the gates of hope . . . a different, some-times lonely place, of truth-telling . . . the place of resistance and defiance, from which you see the world both as it is and as it could be . . . the place from which you glimpse not only struggle but joy in the struggle.
—Reverend Victoria Safford (2004, 1)

Knowledge emerges only through invention and re-invention, through the restless, impatient, continuing, hopeful inquiry human beings pursue in the world, with the world, and with each other.—Paulo Freire (2000, 72)

Choose the quotation you are drawn to, read it out loud, and discuss the following:

- Why were you drawn to this quotation?

- What value(s) does the quotation represent?

- How does the quotation relate to the context of your work?

Values and Concepts Influencing My Program

Think about the biggest hopes and dreams you have for your classroom/pro-gram. What values and concepts are influencing these dreams? Summarize them in five words or phrases that capture your thoughts about what children, fami-lies, and staff deserve in your program, and complete the chart on the next page. Share your ideas with your community of practice. Work together to develop a unified value statement that the group can agree to.

A sample value statement appears at the end of this study session. You may want to use it to help you develop your own statement.

Children Deserve	Families Deserve	Staff Deserve
1.		
2.		
3.		
4.		
5.		

Adapted from *The Visionary Director: A Handbook for Dreaming, Organizing, and Improvising in Your Center*, second edition, by Margie Carter and Deb Curtis, © 2010. Published by Redleaf Press, www.redleafpress.org.

Examine Environments for Values

Study the details in the photos, and use the following questions for a reflective discussion.

- What are you drawn to in a particular photo? Why?

- What do you think the teacher in this program values? What details in the photo lead you to say this?

Field Study

Study the Sample Values Statement that follows to enhance your thinking about values. Finish the Values and Concepts Chart, writing values statements for each column to reflect your values for your classroom/program. Bring your values statements to share at your next community of practice meeting.

Study your environment for specific elements that reflect your values. Take photos of your program that represent your values and bring them to your next community of practice meeting. Consider the changes or additions you would like to make to your environment to better reflect your values.

For Further Study

Use the entire Thinking Lens to continue to study photos of environments that reflect the values exhibited in the following resources: *Designs for Living and Learning: Transforming Early Childhood Environments* by Deb Curtis and Margie Carter and *A Study of Early Childhood Program Environments* (CD) and *Visionary Infant and Toddler Program Environments* (CD) by Harvest Resources Associates, www.ecetrainers.com.

Sample Values Statement

Focusing on Children

We see each child as unique, with individual preferences, interests, and important family connections. We strive to know each child through careful observation, cultivating strong relationships with families and studying child development theory. At every stage of development, children have a profound desire to connect with others and learn about the world around them. We consider all of these elements important when we form relationships with children and their families and plan our environment and activities.

Cultivating Relationships

Strong connections with family members and other significant adults are the foundation for the healthy growth and development of young children. We put relationships at the center of everything we do—cultivating our own meaningful connections with children, helping children stay closely connected to their families, providing opportunities for relationships among families, and developing strong teaching teams within the staff to ensure a quality program.

Ensuring Partnerships with Families

We believe that parents are the experts when it comes to knowing their children. Throughout our program we support and validate all families and ensure that they are represented and included in the daily life of the program and the care and education of their children.

Creating a Homelike Environment

To ease the transition between home and school, we design cozy, homelike environments with elements of beauty and softness to provide a feeling of security and a sense of calm. In our environments, there are places for children to be quiet and alone as well as places for active explorers to use their bodies and senses. We follow a predictable schedule so children can feel secure, yet we maintain flexibility in order to focus on children's individual needs and rhythms.

Planning Experiences

We see the time that children spend in our program as filled with rich possibilities for development and learning. We regularly plan experiences in which children can explore and interact with materials and people to discover things about themselves, others, and the world around them.

Adapted from *The Visionary Director: A Handbook for Dreaming, Organizing, and Improvising in Your Center*, second edition, by Margie Carter and Deb Curtis, © 2010. Published by Redleaf Press, www.redleafpress.org.

Collaborating across Different Perspectives

Review Your Field Study

Share the work and discoveries you gained from your last field study.

Welcoming Difference

One of the biggest struggles of being a reflective early childhood educator is negotiating the differing ideas and perspectives of colleagues and parents. In theory, it makes sense that there are many ways to interpret and respond to our observations of children's learning. In practice, varying points of view can result in tension and conflict when we don't agree on a course of action. Reflective teaching requires not only tolerating the uncertainty that comes with disagreement but also welcoming it. If we embrace the complexity of the teaching and learning process, we listen for differing perspectives with curiosity and respect. Even as we name and strengthen our own beliefs and values, we can challenge ourselves to acknowledge alternative viewpoints.

Opening Activity

Study the following quotation:

> We do not really see through our eyes or hear through our ears, but through our beliefs. To put our beliefs on hold is to cease to exist as ourselves for a moment—and that is not easy. It is painful as well, because it means turning yourself inside out, giving up your own sense of who you are, and being willing to see yourself in the unflattering light of another's angry gaze. It is not

easy, but it is the only way to learn what it might feel like to be someone else and the only way to start the dialogue.—Lisa Delpit (2006, 46–47)

What does this quotation mean to you? Share a time when you tried to put your beliefs on hold in order to see someone else's perspective.

Exploring Perspectives in Observing

Study the following picture for fifteen seconds.

With the picture covered, jot down a few notes about what you saw.

_____

_____

_____

_____

Compare notes with your community—what were the similarities and differences in your observations?

Next, use these questions for a reflective discussion.

Thinking Lens Questions

KNOW YOURSELF

- What in your background and values may be influencing your observations?
- How might your view of children influence what you see in the photo?
- What other factors influence what you see when you observe?

CONSIDER MULTIPLE PERSPECTIVES

- How might culture and family background influence your professional observations?
- What questions might you ask to help colleagues and families share their perspectives?

Activity with Props

Props

Collection of reversible drawing pictures like these examples.

Guidelines

Display the pictures so everyone can see them. Take five minutes to study the pictures individually; then, as a group, discuss what you saw in them. Pick one picture in which participants in your community of practice saw different images. Work as a group to help everyone see all of the possible images.

- How might this activity relate to your work with children? Why is it important to be open to different perspectives?

- How did you go about helping someone see a different perspective? What did someone else do that helped you see differently?

Field Study

Find a moment with a child or children that engages your heart and mind. Observe and take notes and photos of the moment. Write your observation in the format of the learning story of Aotearoa/New Zealand (see the example story on page 7). You can do this in three paragraphs describing these:

1. What happened

2. What it meant to you

3. What opportunities and possibilities you are now considering

Share your learning story with a colleague or family member to gain another perspective on your observation. Bring your learning story, including this additional perspective, to your next community of practice meeting. Use the Thinking Lens questions to consider the value of seeking multiple perspectives in your work with children.

For Further Study

To study the idea of perspective, consider trying some of the activities in *The Art of Awareness: How Observation Can Transform Your Teaching*, second edition, by Deb Curtis and Margie Carter.

Considering Your Image of Children

Review Your Field Study

Share the work and discoveries you gained from your last field study.

Considering Your Image of Children

Your view of children affects everything you do, from the environment and activities you offer to the interactions you take time to have with children. The educators of the schools of Reggio Emilia have inspired early childhood educators around the world to consider how our image of children impacts the programs we provide for them. Educators working in a community of practice can inspire and challenge each other to see children as the competent people they are.

Opening Activity

The statements below contain simple truths. Yet how we see children is not so simple. Which of the statements best describes how you see young children? How do you think each of these views may impact a teacher's work with children?

- Children are inexperienced, vulnerable, and often get themselves into trouble. A teacher's first priority is health and safety.

- Children say and do the darnedest things. They're so cute and funny and always keep me entertained.

- Children need time to develop skills that will get them ready for school and life.

- Children are eager, curious, creative, and competent learners who deserve rich, challenging experiences to develop their fullest potential.

Examine This Story

Study the details in the photo and short description, and use the following questions from the Thinking Lens for a reflective discussion.

Joshua explored the paper in various ways. He wrapped himself in the paper and then wrinkled it and threw it up in the air. He looked through the paper, touched it, and worked to cut it with the scissors. He also tried to tear it with his fingers. He put his fingers through the holes of both pairs of scissors and seemed to study the scissors thoughtfully.

Thinking Lens Questions

KNOW YOURSELF

- What captures your attention as you study the photo and read the story?

- What in your background and values may be influencing your response?

- What adult perspectives—for example, standards, health and safety, or learning goals—are on your mind?

- How might your view of children influence your reaction?

FIND THE DETAILS OF THE COMPETENT CHILD THAT ENGAGE
YOUR HEART AND MIND

- What details in the photo and the story show the child's strengths and competencies?

- What do you notice in the photo and the story that delights you?

SEEK THE CHILD'S POINT OF VIEW

- What does the child seem to be drawn to and excited about?

Activity with Props

Props

Scissors and several rolls of colored cellophane paper

Guidelines

Explore the paper and scissors as Joshua did in the photo story.

- Discuss what you notice about the properties of the paper. How would you describe them?

- What sounds can you make with the paper?

- How would you describe the weight and texture of the paper?

- What discoveries do you make about the paper and scissors by using them as Joshua did?

- What new understandings do you have about Joshua's point of view and his competence after using the paper and scissors?

- What new ideas do you have for responding to and supporting Joshua as the result of your experiences with the paper?

Field Study

Observe and take photos of children involved in focused activities with materials and each other. Bring these photos and stories to your next community of practice meeting and use the Thinking Lens questions to inspire and challenge each other to cultivate strong images of children.

For Further Study

Consider trying some of the activities and studying the chapters in *The Art of Awareness: How Observation Can Transform Your Teaching,* second edition, by Deb Curtis and Margie Carter to study children's competence and their points of view.

Try exploring more materials that you plan to offer children to see what you can learn about their properties and uses. Discuss your guesses about how the children will use the materials. Try offering children those materials.

Delighting in Children's Points of View

Review Your Field Study

Share the work and discoveries you gained from your last field study.

Delighting in Children's Points of View

Most of you chose to work with young children because you loved their view of the world and shared it. Yet the daily demands of working with a group of children, managing ongoing chores, planning curriculum, living up to standards, and reassuring parents all compete for your attention. These factors combine to make it difficult to keep children at the center of your work. In order to delight in children's points of view in this complex context, you must take time to slow down and intentionally work at putting yourself in their shoes. Seeing how children view the world helps you appreciate and support their lively minds and enriches your own view of the magic and wonders around you.

Opening Activity

Read the following quotation and discuss the questions that follow.

> If you have a child of two or three, or can borrow one, let her give you begin-
> ning lessons in looking. It takes just a few minutes. Ask the child to come
> from the front of the house to the back and closely observe her small journey.
> It will be full of pauses, circling, touching, and picking up in order to smell,
> shake, taste, rub, and scrape. . . . The child treats the situation with the open
> curiosity and attention that it deserves. The child is quite right.—Corita Kent
> and Jan Steward (2008, 14)

- What is your reaction to the idea of getting "lessons in looking" from children?

- Describe a time when you were delighted by a child's open curiosity and attention to something you wouldn't have otherwise noticed.

- What helps you slow down and see children's points of view?

Study Photos

Brain research suggests that young children have very flexible brains that enable them to hear more, see more, and experience more than adults do. In order to get a glimpse of what children may see, you can use digital technology to crop and enlarge photos to expose more detail. Study the examples below, describing the textures, shapes, reflections, shadows, movements, and any other elements that the photos reveal.

Activity with Props

You can also seek children's points of view by trying what you see them doing.

Props

Two different colors of tempera paint and three brushes for each person in
the group

Guidelines

After studying the photos, use the paints and brushes to do what you see the
children doing. As you work with the materials, notice the properties of the
paints and brushes, what happens when you mix the paint, and how the brushes
and paints move and work together. Discuss your discoveries with your group.

Field Study

Observe children engaged in focused activities, and take photos of their work.
Crop and enlarge the photos to emphasize the elements that children may see.
Bring your photos to your community of practice and discuss the following elements of the Thinking Lens.

Thinking Lens Questions

KNOW YOURSELF

- What new ways of seeing the world around you does studying children's
points of view offer you?

FIND THE DETAILS OF THE COMPETENT CHILD THAT ENGAGE YOUR HEART AND MIND

- What details in your photos show the children's strengths and competencies?

SEEK THE CHILD'S POINT OF VIEW

- What might the children be seeing and noticing as they work in this focused
way?
- What might the children be trying to accomplish or figure out in each of the
photos you have cropped and enlarged?

For Further Study

Reread the quotation by Corita Kent and Jan Steward at the beginning of this session and try what they suggest: follow a child who is exploring the outdoors and notice when the child stops and pauses to look at or pick up something.

Engaging Environments for Childhood

Review Your Field Study

Share the work and discoveries you gained from your last field study.

Engaging Environments for Childhood

Children's lives are filled with television, computer games, and toys that others have designed for them. They are continually entertained and directed rather than challenged to create and invent for themselves. Early childhood programs are outfitted from catalogs to meet outcomes and regulations, making these programs feel like institutions rather than nourishing places that welcome and engage the hearts and minds of the people living in them. Because children are spending their childhoods in your programs, they deserve much more from adults.

How can your environments reflect the sounds of childhood—cooperative play, big body activities, high drama, messy play, and the importance of family involvement? How can you offer rich childhood experiences in which children can build their passions and attention over time? How can you use open-ended materials to create rather than consume as children learn?

Remembering the joys and adventures from your own childhood is a good place to begin thinking about offering vital experiences to children.

Opening Activity

Read the following quotation and discuss the questions on the next page.

> There is a garden in every childhood, an enchanted place where colors are brighter, the air softer, and the morning more fragrant than ever again.
> —Elizabeth Lawrence (1990, 24)

- What is your response to the idea that in every childhood there is an enchanted garden?

- What role should early childhood programs play in protecting and enhancing these childhood experiences?

Activity with Props

Props

A variety of colors of modeling clay and paper plates to use as a base for your work

Guidelines

Think of an environment you loved to spend time in as a child. Imagine the details of that place. Where were you? What surrounded you? Were you alone or with others? What were the sensory elements of the place? Recall the light, the temperature, the textures and colors. What did you do there? How did you feel?

Use the modeling clay to represent specific elements of that place, or create a design or sculpture to reflect the feelings you had when you were there.

Share your sculpture and tell the story or details about this place and why you loved to spend time there when you were young.

Elements of Childhood in Environments

The following list represents childhood themes that most adults describe from their memories of favorite environments. Study the list together, and reflect on the sculptures you made with clay and the stories you told each other. Which of these elements are included in the early childhood environment you have created?

- surrounded by a cozy, homelike atmosphere

- being with special friends and family

- experiencing magic and wonder

- playing with loose parts and open-ended materials from the natural world

- spending lots of time outdoors in nature, relating to living things

- exploring and transforming

- constructing and inventing

- acting out dramas, power, and adventure
- participating and collaborating around meaningful work

Study Environments for Elements of Childhood

Together, study each of these photos and identify the elements of childhood from the list above. Describe the specific details that reflect the elements you see in each photo.

Field Study

Assess your environment using the list of Elements of Childhood. Choose one area of your environment to make some changes to offer more childhood experiences. Take photos of the specific examples that you add to your environment and bring along the photos to share with your community of practice.

For Further Study

Review the photos from this activity, and reflect on these questions from the Thinking Lens:

Thinking Lens Questions

KNOW YOURSELF

- What is your response to this environment? Why?

- What are you drawn to and curious about?

- What adult perspectives—for example, standards, health and safety, time, and goals—are on your mind?

SEEK THE CHILD'S POINT OF VIEW

- What might children be drawn to and excited about in this environment?

- What might children do or learn in this environment?

EXAMINE THE PHYSICAL/SOCIAL/EMOTIONAL ENVIRONMENT

- What do the organization and use of the physical space and materials in this environment communicate?

- How might this environment strengthen relationships?

For Further Study

Consider studying the book *Designs for Living and Learning: Transforming Early Childhood Environments* by Deb Curtis and Margie Carter, and other books related to early childhood environments to engage in more learning and conversations about the importance of the environment.

Investigating Materials

Review Your Field Study

Share the work and discoveries you gained from your last field study.

Investigating Materials

When you examine typical toys and materials designed for young children, you come to see how limited they are for engaging the lively minds of these amazing young people. Typical children's materials are mostly made of bright primary-colored hard plastic. Their uses are limited. They are often designed to capture children's attention or entertain them. These toys suggest that children have limited capabilities or inner resources and need attention-grabbing, overstimulating, external experiences in order to stay interested in something. These materials do little to engage children's extraordinary sensory capabilities or lively minds. They don't tap into children's deep desires to learn and to hone their skills and abilities, nor do they cultivate sustained attention in their explorations.

Providing open-ended materials and real items to explore offers endless possibilities for children to create, invent, construct, and organize their world. Such materials can be moved, combined, redesigned, lined up, taken apart, and put back together in multiple ways. They can be used alone or combined with other materials. There is no set of specific directions for these kinds of materials. They call on children's eagerness to explore and their natural capacity for discovery and learning.

Opening Activity

Read the following quotations by Alba Ferrari and Elena Giacopini, and discuss the questions about their ideas.

Often people are seduced by materials, which seem to have their own inner life and their own story to tell. Yet they can only be transformed through their encounter with people.—Alba Ferrari (Gandini and Kaminsky 2005, 9)

In our initial professional development meetings with recycled materials, the teachers' first reaction was to gather great quantities and varieties of materials to explore. But as the teachers were invited to observe the characteristics of each material, they began to become more sensitive to the essential quality and value of each small piece. . . . This has helped them to leave more room in construction with materials, to leave silence or pause or breathing room. They have begun to realize how that helps the materials themselves to express what they can express.—Elena Giacopini (Gandini and Kaminsky 2005, 9)

- What is your response to these quotations?
- What do you think they mean?

Examine Open-Ended Materials

Study and discuss the photos on the following pages using these questions to guide you:

- What are the properties and the elements of each invitation of materials?
- What are the possible ways these materials might be organized, combined, or manipulated to create, invent, construct, design, line up, take apart, or put back together?

Activity with Props

Props

Natural materials such as twigs, stones, shells, rocks, pinecones, and leaves.

Guidelines

Study the sensory properties of the materials: their texture, weight, size, shape, color, and fragrance. Explore the different ways you can organize, combine, or manipulate the materials. Play with the materials—create, invent, construct, design, line up, take apart, and put them back together.

Discuss how you might offer these materials for the children to use.

Field Study

Offer a collection of open-ended materials to a group of children. Observe and take photos of how the children use the materials. Bring your notes and photos to your community of practice meeting and discuss these questions from the Thinking Lens.

Thinking Lens Questions

KNOW YOURSELF

- What captured your attention while the children explored the materials? Why?

SEEK THE CHILD'S POINT OF VIEW

- How did the children use the materials?
- What were the children drawn to and excited about as they worked with the materials?
- What might children be trying to accomplish through their investigations?

EXAMINE THE PHYSICAL/SOCIAL/EMOTIONAL ENVIRONMENT

- How did the kinds of materials you offered encourage or discourage the children's engagement?

For Further Study

Consider studying the books *Designs for Living and Learning: Transforming Early Childhood Environments* and *Learning Together with Young Children: A Curriculum Framework for Reflective Teachers*, both by Deb Curtis and Margie Carter, to find more information about the importance of materials.

Studying the Learning in Children's Play

Review Your Field Study

Share the work and discoveries you gained in your last field study.

Studying the Learning in Children's Play

The current emphasis on children's learning outcomes has resulted in teachers offering prescribed activities that teach children specific skills and concepts that they often are not interested in for very long. Yet when you observe and study children involved with engaging materials, you can see that they can learn with excitement and meaning. Providing for and studying these more open-ended experiences can help you deepen your understanding of child development and learning theories and help you plan to provide more of these important opportunities for children.

Opening Activity

Read this quotation and then discuss it with your group. Use the questions to help focus your discussion.

> We want to know what the children think, feel, and wonder. We believe that the children will have things to tell each other and us that we have never heard before. We are always listening for a surprise and the birth of a new idea. This practice supports a . . . searching together for new meaning. Together, we become a community of seekers.—Louise Boyd Cadwell (2003, 25)

Consider the following questions:

- How do you think children learn?
- How do Cadwell's ideas about learning as "searching together for new meaning" and "becoming a community of seekers" challenge or inspire your thinking?

Study the Story of Buttons

Study the details in the photo and short description of ways to learn with buttons. Then use the Thinking Lens questions to guide a reflective discussion.

Many Ways to Learn with Buttons

The children eagerly approached the table filled with trays of colorful buttons of all shapes and sizes. They went right to work exploring the buttons in a variety of ways. Many children studied and commented on the properties of each button. "This one is sparkly." "I'm finding all of the red ones." One child worked for a long while to cover an entire page with many different buttons. Several others placed buttons carefully around the edges of the paper and then made designs inside the frame. Many children made rows, lines, and curves, placing buttons next to each, some using patterns, others with attention to filling space. One child named her buttons a family and made a button house and began to act out a drama with her buttons. Melissa, after exploring the ways she could make lines and shapes with the buttons, used them to spell the letters of her name. Still another child delighted in gathering all of the buttons into a large plastic bag and then putting his hands inside to move the buttons around, feeling them fall through his fingers and hearing the sounds they made. He transferred the buttons from the bag to the tray several times.

Thinking Lens Questions

KNOW YOURSELF

- What captures your attention as you study the photos and the story?
- What surprises you about how the children used the buttons?

FIND THE DETAILS OF THE COMPETENT CHILD THAT ENGAGE YOUR HEART AND MIND

- What details in the photo and the story show the children's strengths and competencies?

SEEK THE CHILD'S POINT OF VIEW

- What do the children seem to be drawn to and excited about?
- What might the children be trying to accomplish or figure out through their work with buttons?

EXAMINE THE PHYSICAL/SOCIAL/EMOTIONAL ENVIRONMENT

- How do the organization and use of the physical space and materials impact this situation?
- What properties can you identify in the materials that keep the children engaged in this exploration?

Study Piaget's Schema Theory

You can also use the button story to study how learning and development theory are reflected in children's work. Identify the elements of Jean Piaget's schema theory that you can find in children's experiences in the button story.

SCHEMA THEORY

Piaget described a schema as a thread of thought that is demonstrated by repeated actions and patterns in children's play. These repeated actions suggest that children's play is a reflection of deeper, internal, and specifically directed thoughts. When children are exploring their schemas, they are building understandings of abstract ideas, patterns, and concepts. Some possible schemas include these (Van Wijk 2008):

Transporting: Picks things up, moves things, puts down or dumps. Uses things like strollers, wagons, bags, baskets, and trucks.

Transforming: Uses materials to explore change in shape, color, consistency, and other properties.

Trajecting: Explores the horizontal, vertical, and diagonal movement of things and self. Makes things fly through the air; moves own body in these ways.

Rotating and circulating: Experiments with things that turn, such as wheels and balls. Explores curved lines and circles.

Enclosing and enveloping: Surrounds objects with other things. Uses self to get inside areas defined with blocks or boxes. Hides, covers, or wraps up self and other things completely.

Connecting: Joins things together and ties things up.

Disconnecting: Takes things apart, scatters pieces and parts.

Activity with Props

Props

A large collection of a variety of buttons and pieces of black construction paper to use as a background for exploration.

Guidelines

Explore the buttons in the many ways you saw and heard the children working with them in the story. After you've played with the buttons awhile, reflect on your experience using these questions:

- What discoveries did you make about the buttons and all the possible ways to use them?

- What understandings do these discoveries give you about children's interest in these kinds of open-ended experiences?

- What new thinking do you have about learning and development theories and how to provide meaningful ways to engage children in learning?

Field Study

Observe and take photos of children involved in open-ended activities with materials and each other. Bring these photos and stories to your next community of practice meeting, and use the Thinking Lens questions to inspire and challenge each other to study the learning and development in children's play.

For Further Study

Research more theories on young children's learning and development, including skills and dispositions for approaches to learning and math outcomes for young children. Reexamine the button story with the information you discover.

Consider investigating the book *Enthusiastic and Engaged Learners: Approaches to Learning in the Early Childhood Classroom* by Marilou Hyson and the online article "Preparing for Preschool Math" by Diane Townsend-Butterworth (found at www.scholastic.com/resources/article/preschool-math).

Seeing Children's Eagerness for Relationships

Review Your Field Study

Share the work and discoveries you gained from your last field study.

Seeing Children's Eagerness for Relationships

Children have a huge capacity for offering support and accepting and benefiting from the gifts given by others, and human beings have a natural drive to reach out and create relationships with others. Yet teachers often try to learn as many skills as possible to teach children how to behave and get along. Rather than focusing on their struggles, study the ways in which children already know how to connect and develop relationships—then you can use those moments to help them.

Opening Activity

Study the photo and story of the rescuing hug (Sheehan 1996) at www.52best .com/hug.asp. The photo "Rescuing Hug"—made famous on the Internet a few years ago—can impact the way you see children's relationships with one another. The inspiring story accompanying the photo describes the plight of premature twins struggling to live in separate incubators. When a nurse puts them together, they begin to thrive. The photo shows two tiny babies in an incubator with their arms around each other.

Go to the website, study the photo, and answer the following questions:

- What is your response to this photo and story?
- Describe a time in your work when you observed children helping and supporting each other.

- How might an awareness of children's innate ability to connect with others help you support their social skills?

Activity with Props

Props

A large collection of newspaper and masking tape

Guidelines

Work in groups of three or four. Use the newspaper and tape to build the tallest structure you can.

Use the following questions to reflect on this experience:

- What specific things did people do and say that helped the group work together?
- What hindered the group's collaboration?
- Using this experience, make a list of the skills and dispositions you think are necessary to work collaboratively.
- What new insights do you have about helping children develop social skills?

Learn from Children

Study the following story and photo. Then answer the questions using the elements of the Thinking Lens.

Almost three-year-olds Sage and Shay arrived at the wooden xylophone at the same time. Shay got the two mallets first and began tapping lightly on the wooden slats to make gentle sounds. Sage watched and listened for a moment before asking, "Can I play with those?"

"No, I'm doing it," Shay responded.

"That's a nice sound, Shay. How about if I use this stick?" Sage suggested.

"Okay," agreed Shay. "We can make music together," she added.

They began to play together, following each other's rhythms.

Thinking Lens Questions

KNOW YOURSELF

- What captures your attention as you study the photos and the story?

- What surprises you about how the children play together?

FIND THE DETAILS OF THE COMPETENT CHILD THAT ENGAGE YOUR HEART AND MIND

- What do Shay and Sage already understand about working together?

- What social skills do you see and hear Sage and Shay using?

Field Study

Observe children working together in an area of the room, and document and photograph what you see and hear. Bring your documentation to your next community of practice session and discuss the following Thinking Lens questions:

Thinking Lens Questions

EXAMINE THE PHYSICAL/SOCIAL/EMOTIONAL ENVIRONMENT

- How do the children use the objects and materials in their play to communicate their ideas?

- How does the environment support or detract from the building of relationships?

FIND THE DETAILS OF THE COMPETENT CHILD THAT ENGAGE YOUR HEART AND MIND

- What specific things did the children do and say that indicated they were connecting with each other and building relationships?

- What challenges and conflicts occurred? What did the children do and say to resolve their differences?

KNOW YOURSELF

- What new insights do you have about children's eagerness and ability to connect and work through differences?

Further Study

Use the photos and notes you've collected to show the children your examples of their abilities to cultivate friendships and be helpful. Describe the details of what the children said and did that reflect their knowledge of how to get along with others. Show the photos to the children regularly, and display them in a prominent place on the wall of your room. Invite the children to add more ideas to the display. Observe the children and consider how hearing and seeing the details of their abilities helps them build more skills for collaborating.

Negotiating the Use of Power

Review Your Field Study

Share the work and discoveries you gained from your last field study.

Negotiating the Use of Power

Adults have all of the power in the lives of young children. We control the time and routines. We are bigger and have more language, skills, and life experiences. We are in charge of the lights, the food, the materials, and the activities that we make available to children. We decide who and what we will pay attention to and how we will respond. We may feel the pressures of working with groups of children. And because some children challenge us, we often feel powerless. The ways we use our power have a huge impact on children. We can use our power to support children's abilities and feelings of self-worth, or we can inadvertently use our power to oppress children and undermine their confidence and competence. It takes continual reflection and negotiation to use our power on behalf of children's healthy development.

Opening Activity

Read the following statement and discuss the questions below.

The Latin root for the word power is *posse*, which means "to be able." Having power means having the capacity to make a difference, to have worth or value. Your goals for your work with children should be for both teachers and children to have the power to make a difference and feel valued.

- What is your response to the idea that the way you use your power in your work with children has a big impact on them?

- In what ways do children have power in your program?

- In what ways do you limit children's power?

Consider Kinds of Power

Elizabeth Jones and Eve Trook (1983) describe the kinds of power adults use with children. The differences they have identified can help you reflect on your responses to the previous questions on negotiating how you use power with children.

Power On

Adults use power to prevent or stop children from achieving their pursuits and interests. This kind of power often oppresses children. It makes them feel powerless and unable to act on their own, which can negatively impact their feelings of self-worth. The appropriate time to use this kind of power with children is when their actions may hurt themselves, others, or materials.

Power For

Adults use power on behalf of children's power through coaching and scaffolding. Using Power For children may be the most engaging role a teacher plays. Rather than seeing your work as jumping in to prevent or solve problems, you can use your understandings, skills, and knowledge to coach children toward their own understandings and competence. You continually decide when to step in and offer support and when to allow children to figure things out for themselves.

Power With

Adults use power side by side with children by playing, sharing, and allowing rather than teaching or intervening in behavior or activities. Playing right along with the children can be a fun, empowering experience for you and the children. You share power in your relationship through the exchange of materials and ideas. Playing with children in this way can help them learn how to share power when playing with their peers.

Activity with Props

Props

A collection of small blocks or manipulatives for two people to play with

Guidelines

One person is the teacher and the other is the player. Role-play three different play situations in which the teacher demonstrates each kind of power while she interacts with the player. The rest of the group observes and discusses these questions following the play.

- What did the teacher specifically do or say when using each kind of power?
- What was the impact of using this kind of power on the play?
- What other actions or words could a teacher offer when using Power For and Power With in these play situations?

Describe Kinds of Power

Use these questions to guide your discussion of the scenarios that follow.

- What would a teacher do or say if she used Power On in this situation?
- How might using this kind of power in this situation impact the child?
- What would a teacher do or say if she used Power For in this situation?
- How might using this kind of power in this situation impact the child?
- What would a teacher do or say if she used Power With in this situation?
- How might using this kind of power in this situation impact the child?

Scenario 1

It's lunchtime, and two-and-half-year-old Lauren lets the teacher know she doesn't want to come inside for lunch. She yells, "I'm not hungry, and I don't want to wash my hands."

Scenario 2

Four-year-old Tameka has been focused for fifteen minutes on designing and constructing a paper house with construction paper and scissors. She skillfully uses the scissors to cut the pieces of paper she needs for her house but struggles mightily with the tape dispenser when she tries to tear off the exact size of tape she needs. At one point, she becomes so frustrated that she pushes the tape dispenser onto the floor and stomps away from the table.

Scenario 3

Eighteen-month-old Lucca loves to find his way to the bathroom, where he usually takes off all of his clothes and tries to sit on the toilet. He also loves to pull on the toilet paper roll, unrolling it until it forms a big pile on the floor or fills the toilet bowl.

Reflect on Kinds of Power

As you reflect on the descriptions you generated about using the different kinds of power, discuss the following elements of the Thinking Lens.

Thinking Lens Questions

KNOW YOURSELF

- What kind of power do you use most often and feel most comfortable with?

FIND THE DETAILS OF THE COMPETENT CHILD THAT ENGAGE YOUR HEART AND MIND

- What details in the scenarios show the children's strengths and competencies?

SEEK THE CHILD'S POINT OF VIEW

- What might the children be trying to accomplish or figure out in each of the scenarios?

- What might the child's point of view be toward each of the kinds of power used?

Field Study

Notice the kinds of power you instinctively use with children. Practice using Power For and Power With when you interact with your group of children. Bring notes and stories to your next community of practice meeting to reflect on the following questions from the Thinking Lens.

Thinking Lens Questions

KNOW YOURSELF

- What kind of power do you use most often and feel most comfortable with?

- How do you feel using Power For and Power With?

FIND THE DETAILS OF THE COMPETENT CHILD THAT ENGAGE
YOUR HEART AND MIND

- What details in your stories show the children's strengths and competencies?

SEEK THE CHILD'S POINT OF VIEW

- What might the children be trying to accomplish or figure out in each of the situations where you used the different kinds of power?

- What might the child's point of view be toward each of the kinds of power you used?

For Further Study

Consider studying more about the role of the teacher in chapter 4, "Bring Yourself to the Teaching and Learning Process," of *Learning Together with Young Children: A Curriculum Framework for Reflective Teachers* by Deb Curtis and Margie Carter. You will find many activities and examples for further exploration of how power is exercised in a classroom.

Assessing Your Disposition toward Risk

Review Your Field Study

Share the work and discoveries you gained from your last field study.

Assessing Your Disposition toward Risk Taking

Teachers have different reactions to the challenging activities children often engage in and what they perceive as too risky. There isn't one right answer in these situations. Some teachers may be too fearful and hold back children from opportunities they deserve and are capable of handling, wheras others encourage or allow risky situations that may not be safe for all children. It is important that you, as an early childhood professional, examine your views about such situations and make distinctions between personal feelings and experiences, coworkers' points of view, and children's strong desire for autonomy and competence. Acknowledging your own disposition toward risk while minding regulations and negotiating with your colleagues will ensure that children in your care are safe as well as appropriately challenged.

Opening Activity

Read the following statement and discuss the questions below.

A risk is something that is possible to negotiate and may be appropriate for particular situations and children.

A hazard is something that is inherently dangerous and needs to be remedied, such as a climbing structure with sharp edges or loose boards that could seriously injure children if they play on it.

Thinking Lens Questions

KNOW YOURSELF

- What examples of the distinction between a risk and a hazard can you offer from your work with children?
- How do you usually respond to children when you believe they are involved in risky activities?
- What in your background or experiences leads you to respond to risk in this way?
- What value do you place on offering children physically challenging activities?

Activity with Props

Props

A long piece of masking tape stretched in a line across the floor with three x's, one on each end and one in the middle.

Guidelines

Look quickly at each of the photos separately, and then get up and move to a place on the line that represents your reaction. Repeat this three times, once for each photo.

X	X	X
Stop this immediately, because someone might get hurt.	Stay close and supervise to make sure the children are safe.	Offer more challenging ways for the children to do this activity.

Learn from Children

Study the photos again, this time for much longer, and discuss the following questions using the elements of the Thinking Lens.

Thinking Lens Questions

KNOW YOURSELF

- Did you have different reactions to the situations in the photos? Why or why not?

- What in your background might be influencing your reactions?

FIND THE DETAILS OF THE COMPETENT CHILD THAT ENGAGE YOUR HEART AND MIND

- What details do you see in each photo that show the children's strengths and competencies in this activity?

- How might your view of children's competence influence your response?

SEEK THE CHILD'S POINT OF VIEW

- What is the child drawn to and excited about?

- What might the child be trying to accomplish?

CONSIDER MULTIPLE PERSPECTIVES

- What are the differences among the members of your community of practice in their disposition toward risk?

- How might your differences support and challenge each of you to think and grow in your practice with children?

Field Study

Notice your responses to situations that you think are hazardous to children. Make notes to yourself about what the situations were and your response to them. Bring your stories to share with your community of practice group, and discuss the following areas of the Thinking Lens.

Thinking Lens Questions

EXAMINE THE PHYSICAL/SOCIAL/EMOTIONAL ENVIRONMENT

- What in the environment or materials contributes to the risk or hazard?
- How does the environment support children to take on new challenges and safe risks?

FIND THE DETAILS OF THE COMPETENT CHILD THAT ENGAGE YOUR HEART AND MIND

- What specific things did the children do and say that indicated they were able to negotiate the challenges and risks?
- How might the activities the children were attempting benefit their growth and development?

SEEK THE CHILD'S POINT OF VIEW

- What were the children feeling while they engaged in challenging activities?
- What might the children be trying to figure out or accomplish?

KNOW YOURSELF

- What new insights do you have about children's desire to be challenged and their abilities to negotiate risk?
- What new self-knowledge have you discovered about your own disposition toward risk?

CONSIDER MULTIPLE PERSPECTIVES

- How might children's families view challenging or risky activities?
- What exchange of information would be useful between the program and the children's families when it comes to offering children challenges and safe risks?

For Further Study

Consider studying the Accident Pyramid on page 199 of *Designs for Living and Learning: Transforming Early Childhood Environments* by Deb Curtis and Margie Carter. Assess your environment to make sure you eliminate potential hazards while retaining enough challenges and safe risks to encourage the development of children's confidence and competence.

REFERENCES

Ayers, William. 2004. *Teaching the Personal and the Political: Essays on Hope and Justice.* New York: Teachers College Press.

Cadwell, Louise Boyd. 2003. *Bringing Learning to Life: The Reggio Approach to Early Childhood Education.* New York: Teachers College Press.

Carter, Karen, Chris Cotton, and Kirsten Hill. 2006. *Network Facilitation: The Power of Protocols.* What Are We Learning About . . . ? Facilitation within School Networks series. Nottingham, UK: National College for School Leadership.

Carter, Margie. 2010. "Drive-Through Training." *Exchange* 32 (4): 61–63.

Costa, Arthur L., and Bena Kallick. 1993. "Through the Lens of a Critical Friend." *Educational Leadership* 51 (2): 49–51.

Delpit, Lisa. 2006. *Other People's Children: Cultural Conflict in the Classroom.* New York: The New Press.

Dewey, John. 1910. *How We Think.* Boston: D. C. Heath.

Fleet, Alma, and Catherine Patterson. 2001. "Professional Growth Reconceptualized: Early Childhood Staff Searching for Meaning." *Early Childhood Research and Practice* 3 (2). http://ecrp.uiuc.edu/v3n2/fleet.html.

Freire, Paulo. 2000. *Pedagogy of the Oppressed.* 30th anniv. ed. Translated by Myra Bergman Ramos. New York: Continuum.

Gallas, Karen. 2003. *Imagination and Literacy: A Teacher's Search for the Heart of Learning.* New York: Teachers College Press.

Gandini, Lella, and Judith Allen Kaminsky. 2005. "REMIDA, The Creative Recycling Center in Reggio Emilia: An Interview with Elena Giacopini, Graziella Brighenti, Arturo Bertoldi, and Alba Ferrari." *Innovations in Early Education: The International Reggio Exchange* 12 (3): 1–13.

Jones, Elizabeth, and Eve Trook. 1983. "Understanding Teachers' Use of Power: A Role-Playing Activity." In *On the Growing Edge: Notes from College Teachers Making Changes,* edited by Elizabeth Jones. Pasadena, CA: Pacific Oaks College and Children's School.

Kent, Corita, and Jan Steward. 2008. *Learning by Heart: Teachings to Free the Creative Spirit.* 2nd ed. New York: Allworth Press.

Lave, Jean, and Etienne Wenger. 1991. *Situated Learning: Legitimate Peripheral Participation.* Cambridge: Cambridge University Press.

Lawrence, Elizabeth. 1990. *Through the Garden Gate.* Edited by Bill Neal. Chapel Hill: University of North Carolina Press.

Lobel, Arnold. 1975. *Owl at Home.* New York: HarperCollins.

Malaguzzi, Loris. 2000. "When We Got the News." In *Brick by Brick: The History of the "XXV Aprile" People's Nursery School of Villa Cella, edited by Renzo Barazzoni, 14–15.* Reggio Emilia, Italy: Reggio Children.

McDonald, Joseph P., Nancy Mohr, Alan Dichter, and Elizabeth C. McDonald. 2003. *The Power of Protocols: An Educator's Guide to Better Practice.* New York: Teachers College Press.

Meier, Daniel R., and Barbara Henderson. 2007. *Learning from Young Children in the Classroom: The Art and Science of Teacher Research.* New York: Teachers College Press.

Miller, Sandra, and Sonya Shoptaugh. 2004. "Reflections on a Journey of Inspiration: Teacher Change in Public Education." In *Next Steps Toward Teaching the Reggio Way: Accepting the Challenge to Change,* 2nd edition, edited by Joanne Hendrick, 241–58. Upper Saddle River, NJ: Pearson.

Paley, Vivian Gussin. 1986. "On Listening to What the Children Say." *Harvard Educational Review 56* (2): 122–31.

Palmer, Parker J. 2007a. *The Courage to Teach: Exploring the Inner Landscape of a Teacher's Life.* 10th anniv. ed. San Francisco: Jossey-Bass.

———. 2007b. *The Courage to Teach: Guide for Reflection and Renewal.* 10th anniv. ed. San Francisco: Jossey-Bass.

Rinaldi, Carlina. 2006. *In Dialogue with Reggio Emilia: Listening, Researching, and Learning.* London: Routledge Press.

Safford, Victoria. 2004. "The Gates of Hope." *The Nation,* September 2. www.thenation .com/article/gates-hope.

Sheehan, Nancy. 1996. "A Sister's Helping Hand." Condensed from Worcester Telegram and Gazette, November 18, 1995. *Reader's Digest,* May:155–56.

Ueland, Brenda. 1993. *Strength to Your Sword Arm: Selected Writings.* Duluth, MN: Holy Cow! Press

Van Wijk, Nikolien. 2008. *Getting Started with Schemas: Revealing the Wonderful World of Children's Play.* Auckland, NZ: New Zealand Playcentre Foundation.

Wenger, Etienne. 1998. *Communities of Practice: Learning, Meaning, and Identity.* Cambridge: Cambridge University Press.

Wenger, Etienne, Richard McDermott, and William M. Snyder. 2002. *Cultivating Communities of Practice: A Guide to Managing Knowledge.* Boston: Harvard Business School Press.